Ecumenism & Philosophy: Philosophical Questions for a Renewal of Dialogue

Charles Morerod, OP

Translated by Therese C. Scarpelli

Sapientia Press
of Ave Maria University

Originally published as *Oecuménisme et philosophie. Questions philosophiques pour renouveler le dialogue* (Paris: Parole et Silence, 2004).

Sapientia Press
of Ave Maria University
24 Frank Lloyd Wright Drive
Ann Arbor, MI 48106
888-343-8607

Cover Design: Eloise Anagnost

Cover Photo: Fragment from a Roman sarcophagus, located at the Museo Gregorio Profano, Vatican Museums, Vatican State.

Photo Credit: Scala/Art Resource, NY

Printed in the United States of America.

Library of Congress Control Number: 2005937040

ISBN-10: 1-932589-25-2

ISBN-13: 978-1-932589-25-2

Table of Contents

Preface

AS MIGHT BE EXPECTED, the first phase of ecumenical dialogue emphasized the common ground between Christians. Faced with persistent difficulties, we have now reached a second phase of recognizing that we must strive to highlight the "fundamental difference." This new stage marks not a regression, but a process of maturation. On this topic, Fr. Morerod writes, "The search for differences may seem anti-ecumenical. But the real threat to ecumenism today is the failure to identify differences properly." The task at hand, therefore, is to illuminate the factors which until now have not been sufficiently taken into consideration in doctrinal ecumenical dialogue. The author focuses on the factor "which has been most clearly neglected"—that is, the philosophical factor—without, however, disregarding "the Reformation's traditional fear of limiting the reception of revelation within a philosophical framework." But to investigate philosophical presuppositions is to envision unconscious presuppositions: "The theologian depends most on philosophy when he is least thinking of it, because then he is philosophizing unawares." The problem with which this investigation is concerned is not secondary or marginal. It touches on a central theme: the nature of the relationship between God and man.

The development of this theme, which constitutes the book's main topic, is preceded by an examination of a preliminary issue: the nature of ecumenical dialogue. The author unfolds his thesis that the concept of dialogue within the natural sciences, the dominant body of knowledge today, leaves its mark in general on all dialogue between different theories and consequently on ecumenical dialogue itself, especially whenever dialogue is not the object of conscious reflection. Thus the positions of three philosophers of science—Karl Popper, Thomas Kuhn, and Ludwig Feyerabend—on dialogue contribute to shaping the idea that some people have of ecumenical dialogue. As a result, it is necessary to specify the ways in which the latter is unique.

The first part of this book, then, which relates to dialogue as such, not its content, shows the impact of contemporary philosophy on ecumenical dialogue (Part One, chapters 1–3).

THE SECOND, MORE DEVELOPED, part of the book addresses an aspect of content, "namely, the Reformation's philosophical presuppositions regarding the relationship between God and man."

In a sequence of chapters drawing on primary sources, Fr. Morerod, to whom we already owe an outstanding study on Cajetan, shows how these presuppositions continue to shape the different currents which profess to flow from the Reformation.

The inquiry begins with Luther, an avowed adversary of any application of philosophy within theology, for whom liberation from Aristotle was the condition for reading

Scripture "by means of the 'hermeneutic key,' i.e., the experience of Christ as Savior." Yet the Reformer's stated purpose should not prevent us from recognizing the philosophical implications of his thought. Cajetan was certainly not blind to these implications: Luther upholds the Scotist univocity which he imbibed from Gabriel Biel, in opposition to St. Thomas's doctrine of analogy. Calvin's formulae are not as blunt as Luther's, but at root, the two Reformers are defending an identical position.

This position has left its mark on modern philosophy.

Here the author refers to thinkers such as Hobbes, Kant, Marx, and Nietzsche, who, on account of their starting point in univocity, were led to uphold on the one hand the divine majesty through the destruction of man, or on the other hand the autonomy of man through the elimination of God.

THE GOAL OF THESE REFERENCES to the past is to unravel the entangling difficulties of the present. Thus chapter 5 studies the recurrence of the same principles in Karl Barth and Paul Tillich as well as in the responses of various Protestant churches to the 1982 document of the Commission on Faith and Order, *Baptism, Eucharist, and Ministry.* Everywhere the idea reappears, more or less explicitly stated, that "upholding the participation of any human action in the gift of grace constitutes an offense to divine majesty." Regarding this idea, Fr. Morerod repeats the question: "In order to safeguard divine transcendence, is it clearly necessary to empty of their efficacy all the actions accomplished by men on behalf of a divine institution? The answer to this question involves presuppositions which none of the responses to the BEM mention, because no one has even guessed at their existence."

The systematic opposition between divine and human action adopted by the Reformers remains largely present in contemporary Protestantism. It has sometimes been identified on the theological level, "but not on the underlying philosophical level." Chapter 6 extends the inquiry into the realm of Catholic-Lutheran dialogue on justification, most notably with respect to the criticisms expressed by various Lutherans concerning the incomplete character of the *Declaration*.

To conclude his inquiry, Fr. Morerod is able to state that "Luther's problem is no problem at all for the theological tradition illustrated notably by St. Thomas Aquinas. Unlike Luther, St. Thomas consciously includes metaphysics in his reflection, so that he is able to avoid a theological impasse. The metaphysical dimension of this question should be highlighted, in order to help resolve the problems which remain after the *Declaration*, and promote a common understanding of them."

BUT AT THIS POINT, one could reiterate the Reformation's objection: you are making the reception of the Word depend on metaphysics; you are stripping away the Word's sovereign liberty.

This objection finds a reply in chapter 7, "Perspectives on Divine Majesty in Two Different Metaphysical Systems."

Following Cajetan, Fr. Morerod quotes Dionysius the Areopagite, "There is nothing more divine than being made a cooperator with God," and comments, "St. Thomas linked theology to metaphysics; Luther explicitly rejected metaphysics, but simply ends up creating another metaphysics from this rejection. Yet both had the same intention: to safeguard the transcendence of God."

Should we be satisfied with this observation? We are invited to examine the relationship between created causality and creating causality. Nobody escapes from philosophical presuppositions. Indeed, to propose an approach to theology starting from philosophy, far from constituting "a scandalous intrusion of philosophy into the domain of faith," "makes it possible to account for Scripture. In fact, do not the Gospels show us Christ sending forth his disciples to accomplish the works of salvation?" Already in 1518, Cajetan had made the same observation about Luther. The result is that "where another metaphysics would obscure the Gospels . . . this metaphysics provides the basis for a peaceable understanding of the relationship between causalities, as expressed in the Gospels and in the life of the Church." In short, "the Christian understanding of Revelation presupposes that man can be an instrument of God."

THUS THE FRUITFUL PURSUIT of ecumenical dialogue requires that differences be investigated on this metaphysical level as well.

This is a demanding program, which will take a long time to accomplish, since those who engage in dialogue are not used to envisioning philosophical problems.

Fr. Morerod points out that the Reformation's mental philosophical principles, still decisive today, mostly operate at an unconscious level. To uncover the presence of the philosophical factor at points of divergence will therefore carry dialogue a step forward.

But the operation of these principles in the unconscious depths of the mind goes together with the rejection of philosophy on a conscious level. In reality, this rejection was more programmatic than real, and the void which it left was filled by other philosophies, such as Kantianism or the Hegelian philosophy of religion. From this double dimension of the mind, unconscious and conscious, a complex speculative situation has arisen which is not always easy to untangle.

Moreover, the fact cannot be ignored that a certain number of Catholic theologians have abandoned metaphysics, attracted by Hegel or too credulously accepting the announcement of the death of metaphysics.

The rediscovery of the metaphysical dimension which the encyclical *Fides et Ratio* demands is a difficult task, but not an impossible one. It is a condition on which the investigation of the philosophical factor in ecumenical dialogue depends.

By now it will be clear that Fr. Morerod's work is of primary importance. It will be a milestone in the history of ecumenical dialogue.

—*Georges Cardinal Cottier,* OP

Introduction

Ecumenical Dialogue and Philosophical Differences

IN ORDER TO MAKE ANY PROGRESS, ecumenical dialogue must unearth the most deeply rooted differences
which separate the various Christian confessions. This
method has gradually gained acceptance, since experience
has shown that the initial emphasis on searching for common points between Christians, despite its benefits, is leading dialogue toward a dead end.

Within the context of the search for "fundamental differences," I am proposing a hypothesis which I believe has
been almost completely ignored: the philosophical difference which from the very beginning has separated Catholicism from the major Protestant traditions, Lutheranism
and Calvinism.

Before proposing this main hypothesis, I will discuss, by
way of example, the impact of contemporary philosophical
factors on the concept of dialogue as such. As for the main
hypothesis, which concerns the content of dialogue rather
than dialogue itself, it relates to the semi-unconscious sub-
stratum which underlies every religious view: the concept
of the relationship between God and man.

I will briefly introduce here the following four points:

1. Fundamental differences in ecumenical dialogue;
2. The existence of philosophical factors in ecumenical dialogue;
3. The conception of dialogue;
4. The relationship between God and man at the heart of Catholicism and Protestantism, from the Reformation to our own times.

1. Ecumenical Dialogue and the Search for the Fundamental Difference

Any dialogue which is oriented toward a specific goal must have some idea of the nature of this goal and the means of attaining it. In addition, each dialogue partner must be thoroughly familiar with his own position from the outset, while agreeing to clarify it as dialogue progresses.

Ecumenical dialogue, which came into existence in its present-day form at the beginning of the twentieth century,[1] and in which the Catholic Church has actively participated since the Second Vatican Council (1962–65), has aroused great enthusiasm. But this enthusiasm seems now to have waned. In 1986, a former Methodist observer at Vatican II commented: "As a grizzled ecumeniac with a wealth of good memories, I have to say that, for the time being, official ecumenism seems to me dead in the water."[2]

---

[1] With the missionary conference of Edinburgh in 1910 and the Encyclical of the Patriarch of Constantinople in 1920. These and other key texts in the history of ecumenism can be found in the following very useful collection: Michael Kinnamon and Brian E. Cope, eds., *The Ecumenical Movement: An Anthology of Key Texts and Voices* (Geneva: WCC Publications; Grand Rapids: Eerdmans, 1997).

[2] A. C. Outler, "Protestant Observer at Vatican II Surveys Ecumenism," *Origins* 16, no. 14 (1986): 256.

Since the 1990s, it has become common to speak of a crisis. Specialists mention an "almost universal" lack of interest in ecumenical themes,[3] a breakdown[4] of ecumenism as a search for unity (sometimes masked by the spread of what George Lindbeck calls "procedural ecumenism," that is, the kind which usually characterizes theological texts written by authors of other confessions).[5] In 1995, however, Pope John Paul II reaffirmed that "[a]t the Second Vatican Council, the Catholic Church committed herself *irrevocably* to following the path of the ecumenical venture:"[6] the

---

[3] Cf. Institute for Ecumenical Research Strasbourg, *Crisis and Challenge of the Ecumenical Movement: Integrity and Indivisibility, A Statement of the Institute for Ecumenical Research Strasbourg* (Geneva: WCC Publications, 1994): "The disappearance of a general interest in ecumenical themes, events, and publications is appreciable and almost universal." The Institute for Ecumenical Research Strasbourg is an organ of the World Lutheran Federation.

[4] Cf. Olivier Fatio, "Le Conseil Oecuménique des Églises doit-il survivre?", in *Pour sortir l'oecuménisme du purgatoire*, ed. Olivier Fatio and Henry Mottu, Publications de la Faculté de Théologie de l'Université de Genève 18 (Geneva: Labor et Fides, 1993), 10 [here translated from French]: "But from all this, the unity of Christians has not arisen which seemed just within grasp around 1961, when the Eastern European Orthodox joined the WCC [World Council of Churches] at New-Delhi and Vatican II was convoked. Since then, we have hardly advanced at all: we have even broken down."

[5] Cf. George Lindbeck, "Ecumenical Theology," in *The Modern Theologians: An Introduction to Christian Theology in the Twentieth Century*, ed. David F. Ford, vol. 2 (Oxford: Blackwell, 1989), 255: "the most noteworthy feature of the past twenty years is the growing dissociation of two different ways of being ecumenical. One of these ways is thematic, the other procedural. The first is defined by its theme and goal, the unity of the churches, while the second is a matter of method: it is interdenominational or transconfessional. Their dissociation is not inevitable. As will be explained in the next section of this paper, the procedural ecumenism of nineteenth-century Protestant interdenominationalism was the seedbed of the thematically-unitive ecumenical movement which came into existence in the first part of the twentieth century. (. . .) Theology has for the most part become procedurally more ecumenical, but thematically less so."

[6] UUS 3.

Catholic theologian is encouraged not to succumb to the atmosphere of discouragement, but to seek ways of breaking through the impasses.

In my opinion, the crisis in ecumenism is due to several factors. The first is certainly the one which provoked division in the first place: human sin, always an antagonist of unity. What Vatican II said of the divisions of the past, namely that "often enough, men of both sides were to blame,"[7] may also be said of the present-day situation. Nevertheless, sin does not explain everything, since men of good will—albeit sinners—are praying and working on all sides to restore unity.

Now that different mentalities have been shaped for centuries, it has become difficult to reach a mutual understanding. The usual ecumenical method does not address all the aspects of these misunderstandings. At first, strongly supported by the popes,[8] dialogue concentrated on highlighting the common ground which all Christians share; whereas the previous spirit of polemicism had primarily emphasized differences. Although this method did enable the birth of dialogue, it cannot adequately foster dialogue's growth.

The methodological renewal, initiated about twenty-five years ago (although there were a few precursors),[9] takes the

---

[7] UR 3.

[8] Cf. John Paul II, UUS 20, quoting John XXIII: "This is what Pope John XXIII believed about the unity of the Church and how he saw full Christian unity. With regard to other Christians, to the great Christian family, he observed: 'What unites us is much greater than what divides us.'" Cf. also Paul VI, Encyclical *Ecclesiam Suam* (August 6th, 1964), 109: "We readily accept the principle of stressing what we all have in common rather than what divides us. This provides a good and fruitful basis for our dialogue, and we are prepared to engage upon it with a will."

[9] Cf. Ludwig Lambinet, *Das Wesen des katholisch-protestantischen Gegensatzes: Ein Beitrag zum gegenseitigen Verstehen* (Einsiedeln, Cologne: Benziger, 1946).

form of a new quest for "the fundamental difference."[10]
This quest must not be misunderstood: "the insistence on a
fundamental difference in the present-day phase of dialogue
is . . . not a regression, but the expression of a process of
maturation."[11] In fact, in 1948, the first General Assembly
of the World Council of Churches in Amsterdam had
already identified the same agenda: "Within this agreement,
we should continue, in obedience to God, to try to come to
a deeper understanding of our differences in order that they

---

[10] The best discussions of this question are found in André Birmelé, *Le
Salut en Jésus-Christ dans les dialogues oecuméniques* (Paris: Cerf;
Geneva: Labor et Fides, 1986), 207–302; the same author returns to
his discussion of this question and updates it in *La communion
ecclésiale. Progrès oecuméniques et enjeux méthodologiques*, Cogitatio
Fidei 218 (Paris: Cerf, 2000), 247–74. He has also coedited a collective work, with Harding Meyer, on the question: *Grundkonsens-
Grunddifferenz: Studie des Straßburger Instituts für ökumenische
Forschung*, Ergebnisse und Dokumente, Eingeleitet und heraus-
gegeben von André Birmelé und Harding Meyer (Frankfurt: Otto
Lembeck Verlag; Paderborn: Bonifatius Verlag, 1992). He is sometimes aware of the danger that this expression could be perceived as
definitively cementing the separations: "For two or three years, there
has been new talk of a fundamental difference between the Christian
churches (. . .). I am becoming more and more wary of this terminology, especially regarding the use of the expression 'fundamental
difference.' In fact, this expression could be understood as being
necessarily negative, and thus as though sealing the divisions forever.
For my part, I prefer to speak of the focal point of the issues which
remain open in dialogue. This is not a negative discovery; on the
contrary, it seems to me to be a step forward, since it allows us to
make an exact analysis of the present-day situation. The task for ecumenism is one of appraising this difference. Should it necessarily
keep its separating character?" (André Birmelé, "Analyse Protestante," in Comité Mixte Catholique-Protestant de France, *Consensus
oecuménique et différence fondamentale* [Paris: Le Centurion, 1987],
39 [here translated from French]).
[11] "[L]'insistance sur une différence fondamentale dans la phase actuelle
du dialogue n'est . . . pas une régression mais l'expression d'un
processus de maturation" (Birmelé, *La communion ecclésiale*, 273).

may be overcome."[12] The meaning of this new approach was clarified in 1987 by the Joint Catholic-Protestant Committee in France: "It may seem surprising that after twenty years of doctrinal dialogue devoted to clearing up misunderstandings and seeking points of convergence . . . the Joint Catholic-Protestant Committee in France has reached the point of raising the question of a 'fundamental difference' in the sense of a 'separating divergence.' Does this constitute a recognition of failure, or even a regression? Not at all."[13] The

---

[12] First Assembly of the World Council of Churches (Amsterdam, 1948), "Message of the Assembly," no. 12, in *A Documentary History of the Faith and Order Movement, 1927–1963*, ed. Lukas Vischer (St. Louis, MS: Bethany Press, 1963), 78. John Paul II also points out that not addressing an issue is not enough to make it disappear; on the contrary, "all forms of reductionism or facile 'agreement' must be absolutely avoided. Serious questions must be resolved, for if not, they will reappear at another time, either in the same terms or in a different guise" (UUS 36). More recently, shortly after assuming his position as president of the Pontifical Council for Promoting Christian Unity, Cardinal Walter Kasper also appealed to the notion of the "fundamental difference," a concept which he favored as a theologian, cf. Walter Kasper, "Le radici teologiche del conflitto tra Mosca e Roma," *La Civiltà Cattolica* 3642 (March 16, 2002): 532: "Un argomento che la Chiesa ortodossa russa adduce continuamente è quello della rivendicazione del proprio 'territorio canonico.' Ma questo concetto rende già evidente una differenza fondamentale. La Chiesa cattolica, infatti, non conosce un concetto di territorio canonico."

This is exactly what Kant said: "If science is to be advanced, all difficulties must be laid open, and we must even search for those that are hidden, for every difficulty calls forth a remedy, which cannot be discovered without science gaining either in extent or in exactness; and thus even obstacles become means of increasing the thoroughness of science. On the other hand, if the difficulties are intentionally concealed, or merely removed by palliatives, then sooner or later they burst out into incurable mischiefs, which bring science to ruin in an absolute scepticism" (I. Kant, *Critique of Practical Reason,* in *Great Books of the Western World,* ed. William Benton, vol.42, [Chicago: Encyclopaedia Britannica, 1952], 335).

[13] "Il peut sembler étonnant qu'après vingt ans de dialogue doctrinal consacré à lever les malentendus, à rechercher les convergences . . . le Comité mixte catholique-Protestant en France en vienne à soulever la

Committee brings the issue even more clearly into focus: "we will address the question of the fundamental difference, in the hope of surmounting the separating divergences."[14]

The search for differences may seem anti-ecumenical. But the real threat to ecumenism today is the failure to identify differences properly. This negligence can lead to two attitudes: either that of claiming that differences no longer exist or that of clutching one's own identity, terrified of poorly identified differences. Both attitudes entail a rejection of ecumenism as either useless or dangerous.

If this approach of seeking differences in order to surmount them rather than simply highlight them seems to have enriched the ecumenical method, the identification of fundamental differences is still in the game.

2. Why the Philosophical Dimension in Ecumenical Dialogue?

Among the factors which "doctrinal"-type ecumenical dialogue has failed to address adequately, the one most clearly neglected is the philosophical factor. A glance at the list of documents published by the various commissions for bilateral and multilateral dialogue reveals that although the main areas of theology have been addressed, one could search for a long time without finding a single text discussing philosophical issues. The present study will be limited to ecumenical dialogue between Catholics and Protestants,

---

question d'une 'différence fondamentale,' voire d'une 'divergence séparatrice.' N'y aurait-il pas là un constat d'échec, et même un recul? Il n'en est rien" (Comité Mixte Catholique-Protestant de France, *Consensus oecuménique et différence fondamentale*, no. 1, p. 11).

14 "[N]ous aborderons la question de la différence fondamentale dans l'espoir que les divergences séparatrice deviendront surmontables" (ibid., no. 2, p. 12).

without touching on dialogue with the Orthodox, which could be examined from the same perspective.[15]

The fact is that the question of the philosophical roots of the Reformation has not been seriously addressed in ecumenical dialogue. I will try to identify the reasons for this silence, and then evaluate them.

Dialogue requires that the interlocutors agree on the terms of the discussion and the acceptable forms of argument. The Reformation, however, was immediately opposed to philosophy. Starting with his very first skirmishes with the representatives of Rome, Luther demanded that all argument unfold from Scripture alone. Since then, ecumenical dialogue with Protestantism has carefully avoided the forbidden ground of philosophy, and remains content to argue essentially on the basis of Scripture and history.

One partner of dialogue can, however, insist on addressing a particular theme. According to Fr. Congar, the Catholic Church gave up referring to Scholasticism in ecumenical dialogue: "The Reformation . . . thus battled a Scholasticism which was eventually left to its own internal quarrels. The Catholic Church's effort during and after the Second Vatican Council has consisted, in great part, in going beyond Scholasticism in order to strive ardently for that which one could call, without unreal idealization, 'the undivided Church.'"[16] In 1972, the Lutheran–Roman Catholic Inter-

---

[15] See for instance the following quote from one who has since become archbishop of Canterbury: "One crucial factor in understanding modern Russian religious thought is the role of Hegel and, even more, of Schelling in the formation of systems" (Rowan Williams, "Eastern Orthodox Theology," in *The Modern Theologians: An Introduction to Christian Theology in the Twentieth Century*, ed. David F. Ford, vol. 2 [Oxford: Blackwell, 1989], 152).

[16] "La Réforme . . . combattit ainsi une scolastique qui fut, finalement, laissée à ses querelles internes. L'effort de l'Église catholique pendant et après le second concile du Vatican a consisté, pour une grande part, à dépasser la scolastique pour tendre ardemment vers ce qu'on

national Commission expressed its pleasure that Catholics had set aside philosophy in dialogue: "In defence against a onesided metaphysical understanding, many Catholic theologians today emphasize a more strongly functional conception which is more acceptable to Lutherans."[17]

Yet Scholastic metaphysics had been the lens through which Catholics recognized the philosophical dimension of the issues raised by the Reformation. As a result, Catholics have had to revise their view of the meaning of the Reformation, which has facilitated a better understanding of the Reformation in many respects, but involves the risk of partially forgetting previous insights.

Contrary to custom, I am going to reintroduce philosophy—and specifically the philosophy which the 1972 report called a "unilateral metaphysics"—into dialogue between Catholics and Protestants. Such an approach can at least be justified as an experiment, in view of its unusual character. Of course, we will have to address the Reformation's traditional fear of limiting the reception of revelation within a philosophical framework.

---

pourrait appeler, sans idéalisation irréelle, 'l'Église indivise'" (Yves M.J. Congar, "Un unique médiateur" [excursus], in Commission Internationale Catholique-Luthérienne, *Face à l'unité*, Tous les textes officiels [1972–1985], [Paris : Cerf, 1986], 279).

17 Lutheran–Roman Catholic International Commission, "The Gospel and the Church" ("Malta Report"), *Lutheran World* 19, no. 3 (1972): Nr. 60. Cf. also Nr. 62: "On the basis of these findings it seems necessary to examine whether the still remaining differences on these and related questions must necessarily be viewed as church-dividing differences in faith, or whether they can be understood as the expression of different ways of thinking. While Lutherans emphasize more the 'event' character of God's saving acts, Catholic tradition is more concerned about the metaphysical implications of statements about salvation. These two ways of thinking are not mutually exclusive insofar as they do not become self-contained and orientate themselves in terms of the critical norm of the gospel."

3. Philosophy and the Concept of Dialogue

Catholics and Protestants are engaged in dialogue. But what is the meaning of dialogue in itself? It is commonly recognized that the rules for interaction between persons or groups vary from culture to culture. Thus it is hardly surprising that differing opinions exist on the nature of dialogue. But when two partners in a common undertaking understand their enterprise in different ways, the situation is not guaranteed to be the most conducive to a successful enterprise.

Just as an individual spontaneously enters into relationship with another individual according to the mode which is most familiar to him, encounters between groups cannot help but be influenced by the spirit of their culture.

I will suggest that the culturally dominant field of knowledge, that is, the natural sciences, has unconsciously disseminated a certain notion of dialogue between different theories. This same notion is very likely to resurface in ecumenical dialogue, especially if the nature of dialogue is not made the object of conscious reflection.

The goal of this study is twofold: first, to draw attention to the ambiguities which surround dialogue as such, and second, to show by this example the value of philosophical reflection within ecumenical dialogue.

4. The Relation Between God and Man: Fundamental Catholic and Protestant Perspectives

The object of religion as such—whatever may be the etymological value of such a definition—is to place man into a relationship with God, in the different meanings of the term. Although Christianity cannot be simply reduced to the parameters of religion in general, it remains true that every Christian confession proposes a certain relationship of man with God, through Jesus Christ, in the Holy Spirit.

Philosophy, too, addresses the question of the relationship between man and God, and its insights do not fail to
influence theologians. This influence is more or less univer-
sally recognized on the theoretical level, with respect to the
interchange between theology and contemporary philosophy. But is the Reformation the only historical exception?
In ecumenical dialogue, the Reformation is treated as
though it arose out of a simple reading of self-evident
Scripture passages within a severely disturbed ecclesiastical
and political context. But what about its philosophical presuppositions? That these presuppositions may have been
unconscious only increases their impact, for what John
Paul II says about present-day theology can also be applied
to the Reformers: "Were theologians to refuse the help of
philosophy, they would run the risk of doing philosophy
unwittingly and locking themselves within thought-struc-
tures poorly adapted to the understanding of faith."[18] The
theologian depends most on philosophy when he is least
thinking of it, because then he is philosophizing unawares.

The main topic of our present study will be the philosophical presuppositions of the Reformation itself, and the
persistence of those presuppositions up into our own day.

---

[18] John Paul II, Encyclical *Fides et Ratio* (September 14, 1998), 77.

PART I

Concepts of Dialogue in Ecumenism and Philosophy of Science

THE NATURAL SCIENCES represent the dominant body of knowledge today. The philosophy related to them, whether expressed implicitly in the work of scientists or made explicit in philosophy of science, leaves an unavoidable mark on contemporary thought, including that of theologians. As in theology, different theories within the natural sciences engage in a kind of "dialogue." We will discuss a specific concept of dialogue between scientific theories, and then investigate whether this concept finds a counterpart in ecumenical dialogue.

We will begin by presenting the epistemology of three major twentieth century philosophers of science: Karl Popper (1902–1994), Thomas Kuhn (1922–1996), and Paul Feyerabend (1924–1994). Leaving aside the differences between these three authors, we will examine whether their work shares a common vision of the relationship between different scientific systems.

Why does our study of dialogue begin with three philosophers? The philosophy of science reflects, and to some extent influences, the mentality of scientists and contemporary thought in general.

CHAPTER I

Popper, Kuhn, Feyerbend

Karl Popper

BORN IN VIENNA, Karl Popper spent World War II in New Zealand.[1] From 1946 on, he lived in London (London School of Economics), and thus was able to receive the title of Sir Karl Popper in 1972. He wielded considerable influence on the philosophy of science in the twentieth century, and many scientists, political analysts, and economists (notably George Soros) profess themselves followers of his school.

Accepting the Partial and Provisional Nature of Theories

For Popper, the evolution of science shows the failure of holistic systems, that is, systems which propose a definitive, all-encompassing interpretation of the world. The constant

---

[1] We will base our study on the following works: *The Open Society and its Enemies*, vol. 1: *The Ascendancy of Plato* and vol. 2: *Hegel and Marx* (London: Routledge, 1945); *The Logic of Scientific Discovery* (London: Hutchinson, 1959); *Unended Quest: An Intellectual Autobiography*, rev. ed. (Glasgow: Fontana, 1976); *Objective Knowledge: An Evolutionary Approach* (Oxford: Clarendon Press, 1972); *The Lesson of This Century* (London: Routledge, 1996); *All Life Is Problem Solving: Questions about the Knowledge of Nature* (London: Routledge, 1999).

succession of scientific theories, especially in physics, has shown that theories are only tentative. Moreover, even in the tentative phase during which it is retained, a theory is only partial: "[W]hatever we accept we should trust only tentatively, always remembering that we are in possession, at best, of partial truth (or rightness), and that we are bound to make at least some mistake or misjudgment somewhere—not only with respect to facts but also with respect to the adopted standards."[2]

It is important to remember that even if a theory has been confirmed in many particulars by experience, it may still be wrong. Although Kepler's and Newton's theories contained many accurate facts, they were wrong.[3] One obvious example is the position of the earth in relation to the sun: part of the reason that the theories with which Galileo clashed had such great cultural impact was that they corresponded so closely to basic everyday experience. A theory is generally recognized as a tentative approximation only when it is surpassed.[4] Furthermore, the progress of physics affects philosophy: Popper holds that Einstein's theory of relativity was responsible for overturning Kant's and Hegel's presuppositions.

The Dependence of All Theories on the Questions They Answer

The reason that a theory which has been relatively confirmed by experience can be wrong is that each theory is oriented toward answering a specific question. Since each question relates to a limited portion of the realities which should be observed, the experiment which is supposed to confirm

---

[2] *The Open Society and Its Enemies,* vol. 2, Addendum, 391.

[3] Ibid., 376–77.

[4] Cf. *Objective Knowledge,* 201: "Only after we are in possession of Newton's theory can we find out whether, and in what sense, the older theories can be said to be approximations to it."

the theory focuses on only a single part of experimentable reality, and proceeds according to only one of several possible methods (for example, one could observe the same human body according to physical criteria such as weight or speed, chemical criteria, or psychological criteria, and derive different views from each approach). To summarize:

> [A] scientific description will depend, largely, upon our point of view, our interests, which are as a rule connected with the theory or hypothesis we wish to test; although it will also depend upon the facts described. Indeed, the theory or hypothesis could be described as the crystallization of a point of view. For if we attempt to formulate our point of view, then this formulation will, as a rule, be what one sometimes calls a working hypothesis; that is to say, a provisional assumption whose function is to help us to select, and to order, the facts. But we should be clear that there is no theory or hypothesis which is not, in this sense, a working hypothesis, and does not remain one.[5]

The repetition of a phenomenon in an experiment is not enough to constitute proof, since a different approach might yield different results. Indeed, "anything can be said to be a 'repetition' of anything, if only we adopt the appropriate point of view."[6]

In essence, no theory can be completely and definitively verified: "Theories are . . . *never* empirically verifiable,"[7] since absolute proof is beyond the possibilities of experience: "no matter how many instances of white swans we may have observed, this does not justify the conclusion that *all* swans

---

[5] *The Open Society and Its Enemies,* vol. 2, pp. 260–61.
[6] *The Logic of Scientific Discovery,* Appendix x, "Universals, Dispositions, and Natural or Physical Necessity" (arguments first published by Popper in 1959), 422.
[7] *The Logic of Scientific Discovery,* 40.

are white."[8] Since we cannot examine all swans, we cannot state with absolute certainty that all swans are white.

Therefore, we should not undertake the impossible task of attempting to prove the truth of a theory. Rather, our goal should be to prove its verisimilitude:[9] a theory must offer more advantages and fewer inconveniences than another. Popper expresses this idea as follows: "we say that T_2 is nearer to the truth, or more similar to the truth, than T_1, if and only if more true statements follow from it, but not more false statements, or at least equally many true statements but fewer false statements."[10] His position implies that every theory contains not only true statements, but also false ones (insofar as the theory entails certain false consequences).

Science Marches On

With such handicaps, how can science advance? It might seem that scientists should hold the most probable theories until a better theory shows up. But Popper rejects this idea, which he sees as disguising "dogmatism"; instead, he maintains that one should choose the most improbable theory. "I do not think that we can ever seriously reduce, by elimination, the number of the competing theories, since this number remains always infinite. What we do—or should do—is to *hold on to the most improbable of the surviving theories* which is the one that can be most severely tested."[11]

The choice of the most improbable theory is associated with the central tenet of Popperian epistemology, i.e., falsifiability. Although it is impossible to verify the exactitude

---

[8] Ibid., 27.

[9] Cf. *Objective Knowledge*, 81: "It is, of course, always possible that the theory may be false even if it passes all these tests; this is allowed for by our search for verisimilitude."

[10] Ibid., 52.

[11] *The Logic of Scientific Discovery*, Appendix ix (first published in 1954), 419.

of a system, its inexactitude *can* be "verified": "not the *ver-ifiability* but the *falsifiability* of a system is to be taken as a criterion of demarcation."[12] One could argue, trifling with words, that to prove a theory false empirically is still to ver-ify it—which is certainly true. But it is easier to hunt down faults than to prove the truth of every particular, which would require exhaustive experimentation. In fact, accord-ing to Popper's final verdict, a theory must be presented as solid for its falsification to have any significance.[13]

A scientific theory should be open to the demonstration of its falsity; thus it must be inherently modest. For this reason, the most improbable theory is considered the best. But there is also another reason: a theory which is difficult to falsify is often a theory which says little, because its scope is extremely limited.[14]

Epistemology and the Evolution of Living Things

Popper maintains that his approach to science bears the mark of reality itself: "In so far as a scientific statement speaks about reality, it must be falsifiable: and in so far as it is not falsifiable, it does not speak about reality."[15] This statement is absolute. In fact, the only absolute which Popper recog-nizes is the effect of errors on theories.[16]

According to Popper, the principles of epistemology are based on an analysis of living things. An animal (and even to a certain extent, a plant) confronts its environment according to the following scenario. First, it recognizes a problem (for

---

12 *The Logic of Scientific Discovery*, 40. The criterion of demarcation allows the natural sciences to be distinguished from other kinds of knowledge.
13 *Objective Knowledge*, 266.
14 Cf. *All Life is Problem Solving*, 1st Lecture.
15 *The Logic of Scientific Discovery*, Appendix i, "Two Notes on Induc-tion and Demarcation ," 314.
16 Cf. *The Open Society and Its Enemies*, vol. 2, Addendum, 377.

example, the intrusion of another animal). Second, it tries to solve this problem, and when the problem occurs again, it relies upon previous attempts, in the assumption that there is regularity in the solution to a given problem. Third, the solution (or the animal) is eliminated if it is ineffective and is replaced by a more effective solution, if possible.[17] Scientific procedures operate in the same way:[18] a problem arises, perhaps because the scientist induces it for the purposes of his research; then by successive hypotheses, he seeks the best means of resolving it. Scientific development can thus be described in terms of Darwinian evolution,[19] implying that all theories, like species, risk disappearing as soon as they are no longer adapted. Thus science's goal cannot be to establish definitive theories.

These principles suggest an aprioristic epistemology[20] which Popper deems revolutionary:[21] strictly speaking, it does not begin with an observation of the entirety of the surrounding world, but with the realization that there is an immediate problem to be solved. We then formulate an a priori hypothesis and conduct experiments. It so happens that this is the way living things behave.[22]

Our knowledge is therefore at once real and fundamentally limited, because the scope of the knowable makes com-

---

[17] *All Life is Problem Solving,* 1st Lecture.

[18] Despite certain differences between the scientist and the animal: cf. *All Life Is Problem Solving,* ch. 1 and especially ch. 5, "Towards an Evolutionary Theory of Knowledge."

[19] Popper's father owned the works of Darwin and Darwin's portrait: cf. *Unended Quest,* 11.

[20] Popper takes his inspiration from Kant's a priori, while modifying it to what he believes is a more radical meaning (cf. *All Life is Problem Solving,* 5th Lecture).

[21] Cf. *All Life is Problem Solving,* 5th Lecture.

[22] Popper is aware, although he does not let it deter him, that his scenario could be reworked by starting the "problem–hypothesis–experiment–provisional solution" circle at a point other than the problem: cf. *All Life Is Problem Solving,* 1st Lecture.

plete verification impossible, and because our hypotheses—like human situations—can be developed indefinitely. A final argument supporting Popper's general thesis is the "mathematical proof" provided by Gödel's theorem of incompleteness. This theorem, formulated by the mathematician Kurt Gödel in 1931, proves that a mathematical system can never be finalized; Popper applies this to all physical sciences.

From the Limits of Scientific Knowledge to the Limits of All Knowledge

For Popper, the limitations of scientific knowledge imply that knowledge in general is limited.[23]

Science comes crashing down. To gauge the impact of this reappraisal of science's cognitive abilities, one must gauge the impact of the hopes which science kindled—for example, with the rise of Newtonian physics:

> Newton's theory was the first really successful scientific theory in human history; and it was tremendously successful. Here was real knowledge; knowledge beyond the wildest dreams of even the boldest minds. . . . Most openminded men, and especially most scientists, thought that in the end it would explain everything.[24]

The depth of the resulting cynicism can be measured only by the magnitude of the disappointed expectations.

Hence, the very meaning of the word "science" must be redefined: "Our science is not knowledge (*epistémé*): it can never claim to have attained truth, or even a substitute for it, such as probability."[25] We must undergo a change in mentality: "I think that we shall have to get accustomed to

---

[23] Cf. *All Life Is Problem Solving*, 4th Lecture.
[24] *Objective Knowledge*, 211–12.
[25] *The Logic of Scientific Discovery*, 278.

the idea that we must not look upon science as a 'body of knowledge,' but rather as a system of hypotheses."[26]

Popper's intention is to reveal the limits of science without being a skeptic:

> [T]he belief in scientific certainty and in the authority of science is just wishful thinking: *science is fallible, because science is human.* But the fallibility of our knowledge . . . must not be cited in support of scepticism or relativism. From the fact that we can err, and that a criterion of truth which might save us from error does not exist, it does not follow that the choice between theories is arbitrary, or non-rational: that we cannot learn, or get nearer to the truth: that our knowledge cannot grow.[27]

On the contrary, criticism of illusions in regard to knowledge aims at the service of truth because the idea of error already implies truth.[28]

Although he thinks the usual theoretical justification of realism has been "disproved,"[29] Popper still considers himself a metaphysical realist who admits the theory of evolution.[30] He even maintains that realism is the condition without which human life cannot be taken seriously.[31] Although like Kant he holds that theories are human constructs, he goes on to say that they must face up to the facts. With his epistemology of approximation and verisimilitude, Popper advocates a "realistic realism" for the experimental sciences: that is, a realism that recognizes the limits of our experimental

---

[26] Ibid., Appendix i, 317.

[27] *The Open Society and Its Enemies,* vol. 2, Addendum, 375.

[28] Cf. *All Life is Problem Solving,* 5th Lecture.

[29] Cf. *Objective Knowledge,* 177: "The commonsense theory of knowledge is disproved as self-contradictory; but this does not affect the commonsense theory of the world; that is, realism."

[30] Cf. *All Life Is Problem Solving,* 3rd Lecture.

[31] Cf. *All Life is Problem Solving,* 1st Lecture.

knowledge and does not seek mathematical certitude therein. As a result, he can say that "[b]y incorporating into logic the idea of verisimilitude or approximation to truth, we make logic even more 'realistic.' For it can now be used to speak about the way in which one theory corresponds better than another to the facts—the facts of the real world."[32]

Platonic and Hegelian Epistemology: The Philosophical Sources of Totalitarianism

Popper's criticism of certain conceptions of science is closely connected to his political criticism. He recognizes that an extremely self-assured science is akin to totalitarianism. Philosophy must carefully avoid sponsoring such deviations. The starting point for Popper's work as a philosopher of science is the modern experience of totalitarianism in the form of Marxism or Fascism-Nazism,[33] which was responsible for annihilating a large part of his family.[34]

Popper rejects the kind of epistemology which insists that it knows the true nature of the perfect state, and which thinks that since many cannot arrive at this knowledge by themselves, they have to be "stimulated." Such a position implies that true knowledge is possible, but not for everyone.

---

[32] *Objective Knowledge*, 318.

[33] Cf. the preface of the French translation of *The Open Society and Its Enemies* (*La société ouverte et ses ennemis*, vol. 1, *L'ascendant de Platon* [Paris: Seuil, 1979], 8 [translated here into English]): "The ideas put forth in this work go back to the year 1919. The First World War had just ended and I had already rejected Marxism because to me, it seemed to create the illusion that violence was justified. . . . In the interval between the First World War and Hitler's invasion of Austria in 1938, I had kept silent about my criticisms of Marx, only opening myself to very close friends. At that time, the only alternative to Marxism in Austria was Fascism, the worst of all. But on the day that Austria was invaded, I took the decision to write this book. It is an attack on totalitarianism and tyranny in all their forms, whether right-wing or left-wing." Cf. *Unended Quest*, 33.

[34] Cf. *All Life Is Problem Solving*, 4th Lecture.

Popper rereads history in light of his epistemologico-
political hypothesis, and enumerates the philosophers whose
epistemology favored an open society in different ways.
Among these, Socrates, Xenophanes, Descartes, and Bacon
occupy a special place. His association of this positivist
philosophical position with a certain kind of "reasonable"
Christianity[35] seems to leave very little room for God.[36]

In contrast, thinkers such as Heraclitus, Plato, Hegel,
and Marx developed an epistemology with totalitarian tendencies, by asserting the existence of a destiny which
applies inexorably to history. Plato especially went astray
with his claim to be in possession of the truth rather than
to be seeking it. This unshakable possession of the truth
culminates in the plan to construct a perfect State where
the individual will be pitilessly forced into the service of a
design which is beyond him. Hegel follows in Plato's foot-
steps: with his totalitarian understanding of philosophy and
history, he is in some way the missing link in the chain that
joins Plato to modern totalitarianism.

Beyond Plato and Hegel, Popper denounces their descen-
dant Marx, who inherited from Hegel an absolute view of
history and knowledge of its meaning. Popper has been disappointed in Marxism, and reality has undertaken the task of
proving Marx's hypotheses false. On a deeper level, not only
was Marx wrong in believing that he knew the meaning of
history, but he was also wrong in wanting to set up a system
encompassing all of reality, a holistic system: "Marx was the
last of the great holistic system builders. We should take care
to leave it at that, and not to replace this by another Great
System. What we need is not holism. It is piecemeal social
engineering."[37] Popper clashes with this scheme on both the

---

[35] Several times in *The Open Society and Its Enemies*, vol. 2.

[36] Cf. All *Life is Problem Solving*, 4th Lecture.

[37] *The Open Society and Its Enemies,* 17. VIII, vol. II, p. 134.

epistemological and the political levels. Unrealistic in its attitude toward knowledge, the desire for an all-encompassing
political system leads to making decisions about what constitutes another's happiness and then using authority to make it
happen; it leads to forcing the facts to bow to the system.

In any case, Popper links a particular understanding of
science to political aberrations. Thus, he counters the stabil-
ity of a Platonic-type science with an attitude of challenging
convictions. To suppress the "idol of certitude" is to slay
obscurantism, both scientific and political: "With the idol of
certainty (including that of degrees of imperfect certainty or
probability) there falls one of the defences of obscurantism
which bar the way of scientific advance."[38] The renunciation
of ideologies—and new religions—is a condition for peace.[39]

Although Popper's "approximative" epistemology chal-
lenges the claim to thorough knowledge of the meaning of
the State, he should not be understood as implying that relativism is the solution to political problems, since—according
to him—the theory of knowledge in systems like Platonism
or Hegelianism is too strong on the large scale, but too weak
with respect to the concrete capability of individuals, subject-
ing them to a plan that they do not choose.[40] For him, relativism,[41] or anti-intellectualism, is one of the causes of Germany's political problems; and the faculty of knowledge is a
condition for freedom.[42] The solution involves finding a balance between two evils, a balance which he believes lies in the
approximative realism of falsification on the political level.[43]

---

[38] *The Logic of Scientific Discovery,* 280–81.
[39] Cf. *All Life Is Problem Solving,* 4th Lecture.
[40] Cf. *Sources of Knowledge and of Ignorance,* III.
[41] Cf. *The Open Society and Its Enemies,* vol. 2, Addendum, 393–95.
[42] Cf. *Sources of Knowledge and of Ignorance,* III.
[43] Cf. *Sources of Knowledge and of Ignorance,* XV. It is the principle of
falsification applied in a certain fashion to politics.

We might ask whether perhaps Popper himself yields to a hasty generalization when he goes so far as to assert that no ideology means no war. He seems to overlook on the one hand that his opponents might consider his rejection of ideology to be an ideology and on the other hand that if ideological factors have played a major role in several contemporary wars, so too, some wars owe their origin to personal ambition or weakness, the desire for enrichment, jealousy, or hunger (even though these factors are mixed with ideology). Original sin is a much more profound, even if generic, answer to this question.

Thomas Kuhn

Born in 1922 in Cincinnati, Thomas Kuhn received a doctorate in physics from Harvard in 1949.[44] He subsequently taught history of science and philosophy of science at Harvard, then at Berkeley, Princeton, and finally MIT (Massachusetts Institute of Technology).

Kuhn accuses Popper of neglecting everyday science in order to construct a system based on exceptional circumstances.[45] His own goal is to present the evolution of science in the daily labor of researchers, where revolutions really happen.

---

[44] We will refer to two works of Thomas Kuhn: primarily his main work, *The Structure of Scientific Revolutions,* 2nd ed. (Chicago: University of Chicago Press, 1970); and then a collection of studies published as *The Essential Tension: Studies in Scientific Tradition and Change* (Chicago: University of Chicago Press, 1977).

[45] Cf. *The Essential Tension,* "Logic of Discovery or Psychology of Research," 271–72: "[Popper] is convinced that [scientific] 'growth' occurs not primarily by accretion but by the revolutionary overthrow of an accepted theory and its replacement by a better one. . . . Episodes like these are very rare in the development of science. . . . I suggest then that Sir Karl has characterized the entire scientific enterprise in terms that apply only to its occasional revolutionary parts."

Why Was Aristotle Wrong?

A personal experience seems to have provided Kuhn with his starting point. When he began his study of the history of physics in 1947, he pored over Aristotle's physics in light of his own knowledge of later physics. At first, he found it to be mostly a collection of errors. Asking himself how such a faulty system could possibly have been taken seriously for so long, he tried to understand it better. It then occurred to him that Aristotelian physics should be situated within the context of the whole, which was oriented toward understanding certain specific points (i.e., questions seeking resolution), in particular, the question of change in quality, and from there, the question of all motion. In this light, Aristotle's physics made much more sense. From this experience, Kuhn derived the following rule:

> When reading the works of an important thinker, look first for the apparent absurdities in the text and ask yourself how a sensible person could have written them. When you find an answer, I continue, when those passages make sense, then you may find that more central passages, ones you previously thought you understood, have changed their meaning.[46]

Consequently, after this episode, Kuhn no longer believed that Aristotle lacked insight, but rather that Aristotle's basic hypotheses governed the results of his research.

Paradigms

Unlike Popper, Kuhn focuses his attention on the ordinary conditions of scientific work. The scientist normally thinks that his science provides knowledge of how the world functions and what rules and instruments can be used to

---

[46] Cf. *The Essential Tension*, Preface, xii.

observe its functioning. The collection of viewpoints by which a group of scientists approach reality are paradigms:

> [I]n much of the book the term "paradigm" is used in two different senses. On the one hand, it stands for the entire constellation of beliefs, values techniques, and so on shared by the members of a given community. On the other, it denotes one sort of element in that constellation, the concrete puzzle-solutions which, employed as models or examples, can replace explicit rules as a basis for the solution of the remaining puzzles of normal science. . . . Philosophically, at least, this second sense of "paradigm" is the deeper of the two."[47]

Paradigms and the scientific community which accepts them mutually define each other: "A paradigm is what the members of a scientific community, and they alone, share. Conversely, it is their possession of a common paradigm that constitutes a scientific community of a group of otherwise disparate men."[48]

The fact that sciences with the same object bear different names proves Kuhn at least partly right. The question is whether these different approaches will be able to be combined; for Kuhn, this reconciliation is still a long way off:

> To a remarkable extent the members of a given community will have absorbed the same literature and drawn similar lessons from it. Because the attention of different communities is focused on different matters, professional communication across group lines is likely to be arduous, often gives rise to misunderstanding, and may, if pursued, isolate significant disagreement.[49]

---

[47] *The Structure of Scientific Revolutions,* 1969 Postscript, 175. This postscript explains the contents of the book, taking into account certain misunderstandings which arose regarding the first edition.
[48] *The Essential Tension,* "Second Thoughts on Paradigms," 294.
[49] Ibid., 296.

To some extent, experts in different paradigms live in different worlds: "[T]wo groups, the members of which have sys-
tematically different sensations on receipt of the same stimuli,
do *in some sense* live in different worlds."[50] This especially
holds true within a single given field of science (e.g., among
different theories of physics), but it also holds true among
different fields, because a discovery which goes unnoticed in
one field may have a major impact in another field.

Normal Science Incorporates Observation into Its Paradigms

Conflicts between paradigms arise because a scientist usually fits every new fact into his predefined box:

> Closely examined, whether historically or in the contem-
> porary laboratories, that enterprise [normal science] seems
> an attempt to force nature into the preformed and rela-
> tively inflexible box that the paradigm supplies. No part of
> the aim of normal science is to call forth new sorts of phe-
> nomena; indeed those that will not fit the box are often not
> seen at all.[51]

In other words, a given group focuses on a type of phenomenon which it approaches from a specific angle. Anything
found on the fringes of this phenomenon is considered to
be outside the object of study, whereas if it were considered
as part of the object, the whole theory might change.

Because of its paradigms, then, a theory may be blind to
certain phenomena which another theory notices and finds
crucial. In the eighteenth century, for example, although
scientists were familiar with electrical attraction, they considered it a marginal phenomenon, because they were

---

50 *The Structure of Scientific Revolutions,* Postscript, 193.
51 Ibid., 24.

unable to integrate it.[52] Every observed phenomenon must a priori conform to previously known laws which risk limiting our understanding of it.[53]

Changing Theories

Of course, it sometimes happens—and here I refer to those revolutions mentioned in the title of Kuhn's major work—that a theory is relinquished when it is shown to be truly incapable of explaining one or more phenomena now clearly recognized. For example, when Ptolemy's astronomy, which provided an explanation for almost all phenomena, was too obviously unable to explain certain other phenomena, it was abandoned and replaced by a new theory.[54] This process does not necessarily happen very quickly, because at first we question the manner in which the theory is applied, rather than the theory itself, and because a paradigm is relinquished only when another is available to replace it.[55]

Changing a theory is not an exclusively advantageous procedure, for every paradigm does allow us to answer specific questions. Hence, a change of theory may entail the loss of certain useful answers:

> [E]ach paradigm will be shown to satisfy more or less the criteria that it dictates for itself and to fall short of a few of those dictated by its opponent . . . since no paradigm ever solves all the problems it defines and since no two paradigms leave all the same problems unsolved, paradigm debates always involve the question: Which problem is it more significant to have solved? Like the issue of competing stan-

---

[52] Cf. ibid., 35.
[53] Ibid., 41–42.
[54] Cf. ibid., 66–76.
[55] Cf. ibid., 77–91.

dards, this question of values can be answered only in terms of criteria that lie outside of normal science altogether.[56]

Sometimes changing the paradigm does not affect anything in certain important applications: Copernicus's cosmology is no better at directly helping us to establish the calendar than Ptolemy's.[57] And it is possible for two paradigms both to be false, as in the case that some scientists consider light as a wave, and others, a particle—while wave mechanics insists that neither theory is accurate.[58]

Paul Feyerabend

Born in Vienna in 1924, Paul Feyerabend served as an officer in the German army during World War II.[59] He studied physics and philosophy in Vienna and then went to Cambridge, hoping to study under Wittgenstein. After Wittgenstein's death, the young philosopher turned to Popper, whom he later rejected. Feyerabend began teaching at Bristol in 1955; in 1959 he accepted a chair at Berkeley and subsequently became an American citizen. He taught at several American universities, and toward the end of his life, he taught at Zurich's Federal Polytechnic School, after leaving California because of an earthquake to live in Italy with his last wife.

Feyerabend is noted for his open contempt for conventions. There are two aspects associated with this characteristic,

---

[56] Ibid., 109–10.

[57] Ibid., 154.

[58] Cf. ibid., 114.

[59] Bibliography of Paul Feyerabend: *Against Method: Outline of an Anarchistic Theory of Knowledge* (London: Verso, 1988); *Farewell to Reason* (London: Verso, 1987); *Philosophical Papers* (Cambridge: Cambridge University Press, 1981); *Three Dialogues on Knowledge* (Oxford: Blackwell, 1991); *Killing Time: The Autobiography of Paul Feyerabend* (Chicago: University of Chicago Press, 1995).

the first of which is a certain relational incapacity. According to his autobiography, events which in themselves make a strong impression left him cold when they happened: seeing the dead in the streets of Vienna at the age of ten,[60] learning of his mother's suicide, and taking part in her burial at the beginning of the war.[61] He summarizes this attitude and gives something of an a posteriori explanation of it when speaking of his reaction to the advent of Nazism in Austria: "[T]he events I did notice either made no impression at all or affected me in a random way. I remember them and I can describe them, but there was no context to give them meaning and no aim to judge them by."[62] Yet in his last marriage in 1989, he would discover both love and compassion. The other unconventional aspect of Feyerabend's character— probably partly connected to the first—is his attitude vis-à-vis academic decorum. Not only did he distinguish himself by often publicly making fun of other philosophers and scientists, or saying that scientists' arguments are not always any better than those of astrologers;[63] not only did he leave a chair at Yale after one year because they wanted to prevent him from holding his classes on the lawn; but he did not take himself too seriously either: "[M]y contrariness extended even

---

[60] Cf. *Killing Time*, 20.

[61] Cf. ibid., 43–44.

[62] Ibid., 38.

[63] Cf. *Dialogues on Knowledge*, Postscript, 66: "Wherever you look you find theories beset by major difficulties—and yet they are retained because scientists have the pious faith that the difficulties may be solved one fine day. So why call this pious faith a 'plausiblescientific assumption' when we are dealing with the quantum theory of fields and a 'silly and irresponsible superstition' in the case of astrology? Let us admit that research is often guided by hunches for which we have only little support and let us apply this admission equally to all subjects and not only to those scientists happen to favour for some religious reason!" Feyerabend explains later on that he does not believe in astrology: his point is to compare it to science.

to ideas that resembled my own."[64] Forgetting what he had
written, when confronted with an unfavorable review, he even
defended himself by criticizing his own—forgotten—text:

> [W]hen a reviewer wrote "Feyerabend says X" and then
> attacked X, I assumed that I had indeed said X and tried to
> defend it. Yet in many cases I had not said X but its oppo-
> site. Didn't I care about what I had written? Yes and no. I
> certainly didn't feel the religious fervor some writers apply
> to their products. . . . Moreover, I could be easily con-
> vinced of the merits of almost any view. Written texts, my
> own text included, often seemed ambiguous to me—they
> meant one thing, they meant another; they seemed plausi-
> ble, they seemed absurd. Small wonder my defenses of *AM*
> *[Against Method]* confused many readers.[65]

Like Popper and Kuhn, Feyerabend rejects systems which
claim to be complete. The reasons for this rejection are
partly similar to those given by the other two philosophers,
and partly different or at least uncertain, especially because
his sense of provocation calls for prudence in interpretation.

The Impossibility of Exhaustive
Scientific Knowledge

Scientific knowledge cannot be complete, for an exhaustive
knowledge of the world is impossible: we would have to
know the world's story before the world came to an end.[66]
This argument closely resembles Popper's arguments
against the verifiability of theories. Consequently, and this
point is common to all three philosophers whom we are

---

[64] *Killing Time,* 141.
[65] Ibid., 145.
[66] Cf. *Dialogues on Knowledge,* Fourth Dialogue.

discussing, "no single theory ever agrees with all the known facts in its domain."[67]

Like Popper, Feyerabend attributes to the theories of ancient philosophy (Parmenides and Plato) modern science's ambition to be exhaustive.

Scientific, Artistic, Linguistic, and Ethnic Presuppositions Limiting Empirical Knowledge

Exhaustive scientific knowledge is impossible, not only because of the extensive limitations of our observation, but also because of the presuppositions behind those observations. This idea intersects with Kuhn's general concept of paradigms, which Feyerabend repeats in different words and to which he acknowledges his closeness. Like Kuhn, he refers to an ancient philosopher to note that presuppositions might in fact guide the way in which we see the world:

> I was puzzled by Anaximander's idea that the sun and the moon were holes in dark structures containing fire. Did Anaximander see the moon as a hole or was he just speculating? . . . Often when wandering around in the countryside I stared at the silver disk, trying hard to make it appear as a hole, or a glare; I didn't succeed.[68]

Feyerabend goes beyond the realm of natural sciences to broaden the application of the theory of paradigms. Art provides him with an example: he quotes an expert in ancient Greek art who states, "No matter how animated and agile archaic [Greek] heroes may be, they do not appear to move by their own will."[69] If cultural presuppositions, whether philosophical or religious, influence the way

---

[67] *Against Method*, 39.
[68] *Killing Time*, 140–41.
[69] G. M. S. Hanfmann, quoted in *Against Method*, 183.

we represent the world, perhaps they also influence the way
we see the world. Egyptian art illustrates the same principle. The short period of monotheism under Akhenaten
briefly redirected Egyptian art toward a figurative style:

> During the reign of Amenophis IV . . . , the mode of repre-
> sentation was changed twice; the first change, towards a
> more realistic style, occurred merely four years after his
> ascension to the throne which shows that the technical
> ability for realism existed, was ready to use, but was inten-
> tionally left undeveloped.[70]

Of course, this last example actually suggests that presuppositions had an influence on representation, not knowledge.

Anthropology makes similar observations. One example
is the Nuers, a Nile tribe, among whom Evans-Pritchard
noticed unusual space-time concepts: they do not seem to
"experience the same feeling of fighting against time," and
they "cannot speak of time as though it was something
actual, which passes, can be waited for, can be saved."[71]
The discovery of America gave European anthropologists a
paradigm shock.[72]

These different presuppositions are all gathered together
in language:

> Whorff speaks of "Ideas," not of "events" or of "facts," and it
> is not always clear whether he would approve of my exten-
> sion of his views. On the one hand he says that "time, veloc-
> ity and matter are not essential to the construction of a con-
> sistent picture of the universe," and he asserts that "we cut
> up nature, organize it into concepts, and ascribe significances

---

[70] *Against Method,* 184.
[71] Ibid., 198.
[72] Cf. *Dialogues on Knowledge,* Fourth Dialogue.

as we do, largely because we are partial to an agreement to organize it in this way" (p.213), which would seem to imply that widely different languages posit not just different ideas for the ordering of the same facts, but that they posit also different facts. The "linguistic relativity principle" seems to point in the same direction. It says, "in informal terms, that users of markedly different grammars are pointed by their grammars towards different types of observations and different evaluations of externally similar acts of observations, and hence are not equivalent observers, but must arrive at somewhat different views of the world."[73]

An Exhaustive Science is Anti-humanitarian

Taking up one of Popper's concerns on a slightly different note, Feyerabend fears that when science seeks to be exhaustive, it may lead to totalitarianism, because "a scientific education as described above (and as practiced in our schools) cannot be reconciled with a humanitarian attitude."[74]

Scientists primarily run this risk, since their formation is a "brainwashing":

> [T]he history of science will be as complex, chaotic, full of mistakes, and entertaining as the ideas it contains, and these ideas in turn will be as complex, chaotic, full of mistakes, and entertaining as are the minds of those who invented them. Conversely, a little brainwashing will go a long way in making the history of science duller, simpler, more uniform, more "objective" and more easily accessible to treatment by strict and unchangeable rules.[75]

Every society founded on absolute rules threatens the individual. Moreover, the danger that the triumphant natu-

---

[73] *Against Method*, 227.
[74] *Against Method*, 12.
[75] *Against Method*, 11.

ral sciences will practice cultural imperialism puts other civilizations at risk, for the replacement of one paradigm by another threatens the equilibrium of the whole system:

> Ever since people were discovered who did not belong to the circle of Western culture and civilization it was assumed, almost as a moral duty, that they had to be told the truth— which means, the leading ideology of their conquerors. First this was Christianity, then came the treasures of science and technology. Now the peoples whose lives were disrupted in this manner had already found a way of not merely surviving but of giving meaning to their existence. And this way, by and large, was much more beneficial than the technological wonders which were imposed upon them and created so much suffering. "Development" in the Western sense may have done some good here and there, for example in the restriction of infectious diseases—but the blind assumption that Western ideas and technology are intrinsically good and can therefore be imposed without any consultation of local conditions was a disaster.[76]

Can We Get Past Relativism?

Feyerabend's view, as presented thus far, seems to suggest that one cannot go beyond the point of juxtaposing collective or individual viewpoints, and that it is dangerous to try to change another person's views. The title and content of works such as *Farewell to Reason* or *Against Method* seem to justify these fears: "Without a frequent dismissal of reason, no progress."[77] The current image of Feyerabend does not seem to be able to get past this statement. But closer examination reveals that he is not attacking reason as such, but a partial use of reason among its many other uses: "*even*

---

76 *Dialogues on Knowledge*, 74.
77 *Against Method*, 164.

within science reason cannot and should not be allowed to be comprehensive and that it must often be overruled, or eliminated, in favour of other agencies. There is not a single rule that remains valid under all circumstances and not a single agency to which appeal can always be made."[78]

In fact, Feyerabend dismisses certain kinds of relativism: "I have great difficulties with some forms of relativism,"[79] and he equally rejects both relativism and objectivism.[80] For him, the incommensurability of systems is not absolute. It can be surmounted by the discovery of inner contradictions in a theory,[81] or when a whole set of factors leads to the total abandonment of a theory.[82] In science, this is difficult, but it can happen. Yet does the same apply to personal or individual rules for behavior? This domain seems to hold little potential for "revolution," or radical change. Feyerabend prefers pragmatic changes through successive light strokes, conforming to the circumstances: "All we can do is to describe the difficulties we have found in the past and under very specific historical conditions, to

---

[78] Ibid.

[79] *Dialogues on Knowledge,* 151.

[80] Cf. *Killing Time,* 152: "Objectivism and relativism not only are untenable as philosophies, they are bad guides for a fruitful cultural collaboration."

[81] Cf. *Against Method,* 226.

[82] Cf. *Farewell to Reason,* 156: "[T]he transition from one theory to another occasionally (but not always) involves a change of all the facts, so that it is no longer possible to compare the facts of one theory with those of the other. The transition from classical mechanics to the special theory of relativity is an example. . . . Entire disciplines (such as the classical theory of the kinematics and the dynamics of solid objects) disappear as the result of the transition (they remain as calculating devices). Professor Kuhn and I have used the term 'incommensurability' to characterize this situation. Moving from classical mechanics to relativity we do not count old facts and add new facts to them, we start counting all over again and therefore cannot talk of quantitative progress."

live with the world as with a friend and to change our habits when life gets bad."[83]

All in all, the later Feyerabend partly rejected the relativism which he had previously embraced, and groped blindly for a yet to be found better view.[84]

Common Tendencies Within All Three Systems

Despite their differences, certain common tendencies emerge from the three philosophers of science we have examined. Since we have approached them as "cultural barometers," we will merely identify these common tendencies. The most obvious point is that scientific knowledge—and from this a characteristic of knowledge in general can be extrapolated—is limited by the fundamental questions that each theory attempts to answer. Theories are not directly comparable precisely because they answer different questions, and because despite certain incompatibilities, they may each be useful simultaneously in the service of a different end. Nonetheless, a theory can still be shown to be frankly inadaptable and have to be abandoned. A second point which deserves emphasis is the concern expressed by these philosophers, that a theory which strongly insists upon its own truth may lead to a form of totalitarianism and therefore be dangerous.

Are the positions outlined by these three philosophers at all related to the views of scientists? The latter are well aware that the truth of their statements is related to a limited field of application, and that, for instance, different physical models which are not directly compatible correspond to partial approaches to reality, with no one model completely

---

[83] *Dialogues on Knowledge*, 153.
[84] Cf. *Dialogues on Knowledge*, Fourth Dialogue (1990).

winning the whole field.[85] This reluctance to be bound to a
single system, thus losing the part of truth provided by a
concurrent system, is probably the source of the fact that in
a 2002 survey of 534 European physicists,[86] 7 percent
denied the reality of atoms (5 percent were undecided),
"only" 43 percent rejected the heliocentric system[87] (9 percent were undecided), 9 percent agreed with the Ptolemaean
system[88] (16 percent were undecided), 36 percent denied
the existence of colors (9 percent were undecided) . . . In
short, "science" may be more of a factor in skepticism than
one might think.

---

[85] Cf. the clear and instructive outlines in Ugo Amaldi, "Verità dei modelli e delle affermazioni scientifiche," in Vittorio Possenti, dir., *La
questione della verità: Filosofia, scienze, teologia* (Rome: Armando Editore, 2003), 116–17.

[86] Survey conducted by *Physics World* (April 2002): 15, and quoted by
Amaldi, "Verità dei modelli e delle affermazioni scientifiche," 123.

[87] For example, that the sun is at the center of the solar system.

[88] For example, that the earth is at the center of the universe.

Popper, Kuhn, Feyerbend's Principles Applied to Ecumenical and Interreligious Dialogue

WE WILL NOW EXAMINE the ways in which the principles proposed by Popper, Kuhn, and Feyerabend appear in theories of ecumenical or interreligious dialogue. This does not mean that the theological positions we will be discussing have been explicitly influenced by theories from the philosophy of science, which is generally not the case. Rather, in my opinion, these positions have been unconsciously influenced by a cultural mentality which is dominated by the natural sciences. This mentality has also influenced philosophers of science, who in turn have contributed to its maturation.

Ecumenical and Interreligious Dialogue as a Comparison of Paradigms

Whatever reciprocal influences there might have been, the theories discussed in the last chapter about the relationship between scientific theories can be easily recognized in many statements concerning ecumenical or interreligious dialogue.

The first example comes from a compilation of opinions on interreligious dialogue, provided by Jean-Claude Basset:

> [W]e can distinguish five fundamental attitudes towards religious truth, all bearing the stamp of relativism; far from

being mutually exclusive, they occur in varying degrees in a context favorable to dialogue. The first and most radical option consists in substracting the field of religion from the criteria for truth and error. . . . The second very common option reduces religious truths to as many hypotheses, which must be validated or invalidated by practical experience. . . . [T]his shifts the focus from the true/false alternative towards the good/bad alternative, in a kind of moralization of faith. The third option is cultural or ethnic relativism, which holds that every religious truth is suitable for a given context: the Bhagavad-Gita for Indians and the Koran for Arabs; each finds the truth he needs in order to live, and nothing is more arbitrary than transplanting a religious tradition into a culture to which it is foreign. Fourthly, there is an existential relativism according to which a religious tradition is not true in itself, abstractly, to the exclusion of others, but only for him who lives by it; this does not prevent another tradition from being true for another believer, or for the same person at a different moment of his life. . . . Finally, a fifth position rests upon the distinction between the ultimate reality from which religious life draws its essence and towards which it tends, and the expression of this reality in the human response.[1]

---

[1] "[N]ous pouvons distinguer cinq attitudes fondamentales à l'égard de la vérité religieuse, toutes empreintes de relativisme; loin de s'exclure mutuellement, elles interviennent à un degré ou à un autre dans un contexte favorable au dialogue. La première option, la plus radicale, consiste à soustraire le domaine religieux aux critères de la vérité et de l'erreur. . . . La deuxième option, très courante, réduit les vérités religieuses à autant d'hypothèses qui demandent à être confirmées ou infirmées par la pratique . . . elle opère un glissement de l'alternative vrai/faux vers l'alternative bien/mal, une sorte de moralisation de la foi. La troisième option est le relativisme culturel ou ethnique selon lequel chaque vérité religieuse est appropriée à un contexte donné: la Bhagavad-Gita pour les Indiens et le Coran pour les Arabes, chacun trouve la vérité dont il a besoin pour vivre, et rien n'est plus arbitraire que de transplanter une tradition religieuse dans une culture qui lui est étrangère. . . . En quatrième lieu, il y a un relativisme existentiel pour lequel une tradition religieuse n'est pas

The attitudes presented by Basset manifest certain familiar presuppositions: no system can claim to be strictly true; statements (like paradigms) depend on their personal and cultural context; every theory is only an imperfect formulation of experience. Basset summarizes his own foundational principle: "All ecumenical dialogue rests upon ecclesiological pluralism and a certain relativism in relation to the expression of truth."[2]

Religious Theories Cannot Be Completely Verified

Keeping in mind Karl Popper's remarks about the non-verifiability of scientific theories (which can never be 100 percent verified), we find a very similar idea in Rabbi Irving Greenberg's theory of interreligious dialogue:

> There is a variety of possibilities. It may be that the pluralists realize that they do not have 100% of the truth—or that faith cannot exhaust 100% of the experience of the divine. Or, pluralism may lead to a more modest admission. One's (inside) system may incorporate 100% of the divine encounter, but the pluralists recognize that this encounter does not cover 100% of the time that the encounter is available or 100% of the human situations to which it speaks. This leaves room for other experiences to take place. There may even be a more modest limitation (if you will, soft pluralism). One may claim

---

vraie en soi, abstraitement, à l'exclusion des autres, mais vraie pour celui qui en vit; cela n'interdit pas qu'une autre tradition soit vraie pour un autre croyant, ou pour le même, à un autre moment de sa vie. . . . Il est enfin une cinquième position qui repose sur une distinction fondamentale entre la réalité ultime d'où la vie religieuse tire son essence et vers laquelle elle tend, et l'expression de cette vérité dans la réponse humaine." (Jean-Claude Basset, *Le dialogue interreligieux: Histoire et avenir*, Cogitatio Fidei 197 [Paris: Cerf, 1996], 266–68).

2 Ibid., 273.

that [in] one's system knowledge of the truth is absolute and that the ability of this truth to cover all situations is also absolute, but still it cannot reach 100% of the people, whether it be for cultural or other reasons.[3]

Religious Traditions as Partial Adaptations to an Environment

Popper—together with Kuhn and Feyerabend, but in different words—considers science as the search for adaptation to the current environment, so that its assertions are partly limited within time and space. A similar idea surfaces in a document of dialogue between Lutherans and Methodists, which describes the historical institutions as at once adequate and inadequate."[4]

Popper's evolutionary outline clearly reappears in John Hick:[5]

> There is indeed a fixed basis or, better, a fixed starting point, for christian belief and worship; but proceeding from that starting point there is a still unfinished history of change as the christian way has been followed through the centuries, meeting new human circumstances and new intellectual climates.[6]

In unfolding its official vision of ecumenism, the Federation of Swiss Protestant Churches (FSPC) begins from the

---

[3] Rabbi Irving Greenberg, "Seeking the Religious Roots of Pluralism: In the Image of God and Covenant," *Journal of Ecumenical Studies* 34, no. 3 (Summer 1997): 389.

[4] Cf. Lutheran-Methodist Joint Commission, *The Church, Community of Grace* (Geneva: Lutheran World Federation; Lake Junaluska, NC: World Methodist Council, 1984).

[5] Cf. my article, "La relation entre les religions selon John Hick," *Nova et Vetera* 75 (2000): 35–62.

[6] John Hick, *God and the Universe of Faiths: Essays in the Philosophy of Religion* (London: Macmillan, 1973), 111.

principle of the relativity of positions: "The ecumenical undertaking is born out of a self-critical view which makes us aware of our relativity. . . . No Church fully possesses knowledge of the Truth, nor the fullness of the Church, nor that of her ministry."[7] This relativity results from a dependence on context: "[T]he same declaration or . . . the same action may correspond to the Truth in a given situation and contradict it in another context."[8]

Totalitarianism

Some theologians conceive of a connection between doctrinal unity and the inherent danger of authoritarianism, although they usually do not refer to Popper's theory.[9] Discussing the theory of ecumenical dialogue, Fr. Christian Duquoc explicitly states that ecumenism cannot aim for a uniting of churches, since to do so would be totalitarian:

[E]cumenism has effectively created an irreversible current: a current of theological thinking that can no longer be restricted to the limits of a single confession or of a single historical church. This thinking, arising from a practical experience that very often precedes the goodwill of the apparatus, undermines the unitary ideology which is partly

---

7 "L'engagement oecuménique naît du regard autocritique qui nous fait prendre conscience de notre relativité. . . . Aucune Église ne possède pleinement la connaissance de la Vérité, ni la plénitude de l'Église, ni celle de son ministère" (Federation of Swiss Protestant Churches [Fédération des Églises Protestantes de Suisse], *Lignes directrices de l'action oecuménique* [1994, manual published and distributed by FSPC], I.4).

8 "Une même déclaration ou . . . une même action peuvent correspondre à la Vérité dans une situation déterminée et la contredire dans un autre contexte" (ibid., I.5).

9 This connection, however, can be found in Elmar Klinger, "Macht und Dialog, Die grundlegende Bedeutung des Pluralismus in der Kirche," in *Dialog als Selbstvollzug der Kirche?*, ed. Gebhard Fürst (Freiburg: Herder, 1997), 151.

connected with violence and which has produced so many
misdeeds and crimes in the history of Christianity.[10]

The very idea of a specific ecclesiological model—in this
instance the sacramental model—is perceived as violence:

> Despite the recognition that the separated churches are
> churches, despite the acceptance of the right to public
> opinion within Catholicism, they suffer violence, since the
> model of unity is already conveyed in a sacramental way;
> the relationship between the visible and the invisible is
> accomplished in the Catholic institution as it is realized in
> the Eucharist. . . . Behind this issue appears the violence
> inherent in presenting an institution which incarnates the
> transcendent Truth. The transcendental qualities of the
> Church which are professed in the Creed abolish neither
> the divisions among churches nor their internal tensions.[11]

---

[10] "L'oecuménisme a en effet créé un courant irréversible: celui d'une
pensée théologique qui ne peut désormais se restreindre aux limites
d'une seule confession ou d'une seule Église historique. Cette pensée,
issue d'une pratique qui bien souvent précède le bon vouloir des
appareils, sape l'idéologie unitaire qui a partie liée avec la violence et
qui a produit tant de méfaits et de crimes dans l'histoire du christian-
isme" (Christian Duquoc, Des Églises provisoires: Essai d'ecclesiologie
oecuménique, Théologies [Paris: Cerf, 1985], 9). Cf. also ibid., 7–8
[here translated from French]: "the multiplicity of churches, far from
having to be marginalized as an unfortunate accident of our history,
forms on the contrary the starting point for theological thought on
ecclesiology. Forgetting the empirical multiplicity orients us towards
idealistic thinking; then the Church we are talking about is no longer
our easily-recognized historical Church, but its ideality. There is only
a short distance from ideality to the imposition of norms on concrete
reality, and from the imposition of norms, to repressive practices. If
the ideal Church is one and holy, and if this perfection is projected
onto an empirical Church, this Church has no choice but to excom-
municate the churches which have no right to this privileged relationship with ideality. Our history has illustrated the practical and
violent excesses of this kind of thinking."

[11] "Malgré la reconnaissance que les Église séparées sont des Églises, malgré l'acceptation du droit à une opinion publique en catholicisme,

The Future of Dialogue
on the Basis of These Premises

On the basis of the above premises, what is the future of ecumenical dialogue (and, mutatis mutandis, of interreligious dialogue)?

For the FSPC, ecumenism cannot progress beyond the plurality of confessions: "The goal is not standardization, but a plurality which is confessional, trans-confessional, and contextual with regard to the expressions of the Church which mutually challenge each other."[12] Of course this view of ecumenism is not unanimously held by Reformed theologians,[13] but the fact that it was clearly affirmed as the official position of Swiss Protestants shows at least that it exists in full force. Along similar lines, David Tracy thinks that dreams of universalism must be renounced, and that "the particularity of each tradition will gain in intensity."[14] For Jean-Claude Basset, in the final analysis, the current shape of Western civilization

---

violence leur est faite puisque le modèle de l'unité est déjà donné de façon sacramentelle: l'articulation entre le visible et l'invisible s'accomplit dans l'institution catholique comme elle se réalise dans l'eucharistie. . . . Derrière cette problématique se dessine la violence immanente à la présentation d'une institution incarnant la Vérité transcendante. Les qualités transcendantales de l'Église confessées dans le Symbole de foi ne suppriment ni les divisions des Eglises, ni les tensions internes" (Christian Duquoc, *Je crois en l'Église: Précarité institutionnelle et Règne de Dieu,* "Théologies" [Paris: Cerf, 1999], 134).

12 "Le but n'est pas une uniformisation, mais une pluralité confessionnelle, transconfessionnelle et contextuelle d'expressions de l'Église qui s'interpellent mutuellement" (FSPC, *Lignes directrices,* I.6).

13 In 1984, when the international commission on dialogue between Anglicans and the Reformed Churches contemplated such a view of ecumenism, it was rejected. Cf. Anglican-Reformed International Commission, *God's Reign and Our Unity: The Report of the Anglican-Reformed International Commission 1984* (London: SPCK; Edinburgh: The Saint Andrew Press, 1984), nos. 106 and 110, 67–69.

14 Cf. David Tracy, *The Analogical Imagination: Christian Theology and the Culture of Pluralism* (New York: Crossroad, 1987), 450: "At least for those who hold to the ideal of an analogical imagination, the

is expressed by the abandonment of all metaphysical discourse and the renunciation by the social sciences of any global view of reality and humanity, for the sake of a sectional analysis whose main criterion is internal coherence. . . . In religious life, pluralism entails the disappearance of a recognized scale of values in favor of more or less autonomous institutions and thus the relativization of every system of thought and every practice, religious or not. This relativization is twofold: every system is only one among others, and it has only a relative value in the life of the individual; indeed, it has become rare for someone to be ready to die for his faith.[15]

---

dreams—the all too universal dreams—of Arnold Toynbee and other abstract universalists will not prove the route to follow. Rather the particularity of each tradition will gain in intensity as its own focal meaning becomes clearer to itself and others, as its ordered relationships for the whole come more clearly into analogical view."

[15] "Cela [le relativisme] se traduit par l'abandon de tout discours métaphysique et le renoncement des sciences humaines à toute vision globale de la réalité et de l'humanité, au profit d'une analyse sectorielle dont le critère principal est la cohérence interne. . . . Dans la vie religieuse, le pluralisme entraîne la disparition d'une échelle des valeurs reconnue, au profit d'institutions plus ou moins autonomes, et donc la relativisation de tout système de pensée et de toute pratique, religieuse ou non. La relativisation est double: tout système n'est qu'un parmi d'autres et il n'est qu'une valeur relative dans la vie de l'individu; en effet, il est devenu rare que l'on soit prêt à mourir pour sa foi." (Jean-Claude Basset, *Le dialogue interreligieux*, 264).

CHAPTER 3

The Nature of Scientific Dialogue vs. Religious Dialogue

Parallels Between Scientific and Religious Dialogue

WE HAVE ENDEAVORED to show the parallels between certain conceptions of scientific dialogue and dialogue among religious systems. The main elements are the use of paradigms as foundational questions which determine the worth and limits of a system and the idea that no system is complete.

Before discussing the difference between kinds of knowledge—scientific knowledge and the knowledge of faith—we should comment on the specifically theological view of dialogue. For example, if it is true that each religion addresses particular questions preferentially, it remains to be seen whether all fundamental questions are equivalent, especially in the case of a revelation where the questions are formulated not only by man, but by God first of all. The claim that all religions can be seen comprehensively from a self-styled "scientific" or neutral point of view risks not doing justice to any of the religions under consideration.

Moreover, the assertion that no system possesses the whole truth is often intended to mean that no system can deny all truth to the others. Indeed the Catholic Church, for example, does not deny that elements of truth or sanctification are found in other Christian denominations or religions, but this does not mean that she should cease affirming that she contains the entirety of the means of salvation:

> [S]ome, even very many, of the most significant elements and endowments which together go to build up and give life to the Church itself, can exist outside the visible boundaries of the Catholic Church: the written Word of God; the life of grace; faith, hope and charity, with the other interior gifts of the Holy Spirit, as well as visible elements. All of these, which come from Christ and lead back to him, belong by right to the one Church of Christ. . . . It follows that the separated churches and communities as such, though we believe they suffer from the defects already mentioned, have been by no means deprived of significance and importance in the mystery of salvation. For the Spirit of Christ has not refrained from using them as means of salvation which derive their efficacy from the very fullness of grace and truth entrusted to the Catholic Church. . . . For it is only through Christ's Catholic Church alone, which is the universal help towards salvation, that the fullness of the means of salvation can be obtained.[1]

In this context, to say that the Catholic Church possesses the fullness of truth is not to deny all truth to non-Catholics (nor to deny them the additional gift of the beatific vision); for in this instance, the systems or communities in question are not completely exterior to each other, but more or less completely integrated into the same work of salvation offered to all human beings in Christ.

Comparison of Scientific Knowledge and the Knowledge from Faith

To grasp the limits of what theories of the philosophy of science can bring to theology, we must define the differences

---

[1] UR 3.

between the two types of knowledge. This is especially important, since the philosophy of science as presented here does not encompass the whole of philosophy—it asks very few properly metaphysical questions.

Theories of scientific knowledge derive their strength primarily from the widespread notion that scientific knowledge is the sure and trustworthy form of knowledge, the one which achieves concrete results and provides real help—unlike religion or philosophy. This far-reaching assumption combines with a growing awareness of the limits of scientific progress to arrive at the following syllogism:

1. (Natural) science is the most powerful form of knowledge.
2. This knowledge is limited.
3. Therefore all our knowledge is limited.

The major premise (1) of this argument is the one that needs to be challenged, by distinguishing between various types of knowledge.

Failure to grasp the difference between scientific knowledge and knowledge from faith can lead to absurdities such as calculating the age of God on the basis of physics,[2] or inaccuracies like the idea that all religions are equal because meditation always activates the same part of the brain.[3] Both

---

[2] Cf. Gerald Grushow, *Science of God* (Virginia Beach: Starway Scientific Press, 2001), 8.

[3] Cf. Andrew Newberg, Eugene D'Aquili, and Vincent Rause, *Why God Won't Go Away: Brain Science and the Biology of Belief* (New York: Ballantine Books, 2001). Their reasoning proceeds in stages. The authors begin by affirming that mystical experiences are associated with observable neurological activities, in all religions (cf. p. 36: "Our experiment with Tibetan meditators and Franciscan nuns showed that the events they considered spiritual were, in fact, associated with observable neurological activity"; p. 147: "The transcendent state we call Absolute Unitary Being refers to states known by

types of knowledge appeal to reason to organize known facts
which originate not from reason itself, but from the senses
(in the case of science) or from divine revelation (in the case
of faith). In both cases, the data are developed through reason: science reasons on the basis of sense knowledge, which is
usually passed on by instruments and built up with the help
of theories, whereas knowledge from faith reflects on what
God has transmitted through created means (Church, Scripture). Science and faith thus constitute two rational forms of
knowledge, neither of which can be simply equated with reason, and both of which must be distinguished with reference
to their origins, objects, and the types of questions they ask.

St. Thomas Aquinas compares the kinds of certitude
proper to science and faith (by "science" he means the
rational knowledge that is based on reliable sense knowledge, which remains at the root of the more sophisticated
definitions in use today):

> [O]n the part of its cause . . . a thing which has a more cer-
> tain cause, is itself more certain. In this way faith is more

---

various names in different cultures—the Tao, Nirvana, the Unio
Mystica, Brahman-atman—but which every persuasion describes in
strikingly similar terms. It is a state of pure awareness, a clear and
vivid consciousness of no-thing. Yet it is also a sudden, vivid consciousness of everything as an undifferentiated whole"). On this "scientific" basis, the authors affirm the identity of all religions (cf. p.
165: "If we are right, if religions and the literal Gods they define are
in fact interpretations of transcendent experience, then all interpretations of god are rooted, ultimately, in the same experience of transcendent unity. This holds true whether this ultimate reality actually
exists, or is only a neurological perception generated by an unusual
brain state. All religions, therefore, are kin. None of them can exclusively own the realist reality, but all of them, in their best, steer the
heart and the mind in the right direction"; p. 168: "The neurology
of transcendence can, at the very least, provide a biological framework within which all religions can be reconciled'"). *Sciences et
Avenir* (September 2003): 12–13.

certain than those three virtues [among which is science], because it is founded on the Divine truth, whereas the aforesaid three virtues are based on human reason. Secondly, certitude may be considered on the part of the subject, and thus the more a man's intellect lays hold of a thing, the more certain it is. In this way, faith is less certain, because matters of faith are above the human intellect, whereas the objects of the aforesaid three virtues are not. Since, however, a thing is judged simply with regard to its cause, but relatively, with respect to a disposition on the part of the subject, it follows that faith is more certain simply, while the others are more certain relatively, i.e. for us.[4]

The principles are clear: science is more obvious because its knowledge is more immediate; faith is not obvious (which belongs to its very definition because its object is unseen),[5] but it is certain with respect to its cause, which is God's revelation of Himself.

An accurate distinction between the types of knowledge suggests at least that prudence is required in applying to theology theories concerning the certitude of scientific knowledge. The real goal of ecumenical dialogue is not a comparison of human theories such as scientific theories. Ecumenical dialogue is a dialogue in which all the churches or communities presume the definitive and sure Christian revelation as their common base, and in which the dispute is centered on interpretation. This does not mean that the dispute can be easily settled, but at least that it does not fall into the same category as conflicts between scientific theories. I do not propose to resolve here the question of the debate between interpretations, to which I will devote part of a future work.

---

[4] IIa IIae, q. 4, a. 8.
[5] Cf. IIa IIAe, q. 4, a. 1.

Conclusions About the
Conceptions of Dialogue

Despite their notable differences, Popper, Kuhn, and Feyerabend are united in illustrating a growing recognition of
the limits of scientific knowledge, though certainly without
completely denying its value. The chief determining factor
in this recognition seems to be the division of the sciences
into different systems which are not totally compatible.
Moreover, two partly incompatible systems may both be
supported by the same experimental base, making it
extremely complicated to choose between them. Each different system may be valuable in relation to the goal it pur-
sues, which is to answer a specific question; different questions lead to different perceptions of the same object.

This situation—among other factors—engenders the
doubt in contemporary culture as to the possibility of
affirming that one system is more true than another, or
even that one of the systems is false. The same doubt surfaces in the domain of religion, partly based on similar
arguments: each system answers a question asked in a specific time and place, and cannot be directly compared to
another system whose original question is different. Total
relativism may result, making it impossible to progress
beyond the statement that what is true for one may not be
true for another. In such a view, ecumenical (and interreligious) dialogue no longer consists in searching for unity as
its end, but only in amicably discovering what everyone
else thinks.

There is certainly an element of truth in the statement
that every religious system is tied to certain questions
which depend on historically situated facts (think of the
connection between the Christian Easter event and the
slavery of the Hebrews in Egypt). Yet if this link indicates a

total dependence, it becomes impossible for God to reveal Himself to human beings in such a way that they can subsequently know Him and be in communion with Him in different times, places, and cultures. The same applies even to the specificity of revelation and faith in relation to purely human forms of knowledge; and this issue is even deeper than any theory of ecumenical dialogue.

The last word on this subject belongs to St. Irenaeus of Lyons, responding to the Gnostics of the second century, who held that the Church's faith is dependent on what Christ and the Apostles were able to say to the crowds according to their capacity to understand.[6] In his day, then, the notion had already arisen that the faith is limited by the questions asked and the answers that the hearers are capable of receiving. Irenaeus clearly understood that if such is the case, revelation can add nothing to the opinions already existing in the world:

> But as some of these men impudently assert that the apostles, when preaching among the Jews, could not declare to them another god besides Him in whom they (their hearers) believed, we say to them, that if the apostles used to speak to people in accordance with the opinion instilled into them of old, no one learned the truth from them, nor, at a much earlier date, from the Lord; for they say that He did Himself speak after the same fashion. Wherefore neither do these men themselves know the truth; but since such was their opinion regarding God, they had just received doctrine as they were able to hear it. According to this manner of speaking, therefore, the rule of truth can be with nobody; but all learners will ascribe this practice to all [teachers], that just as every person thought, and as far as his capability extended, so was also the language addressed to him. But the advent of the Lord will appear superfluous

---

[6] Cf. Irenaeus of Lyons, *Adversus Haereses*, Book 3, ch. 5, no. 1.

and useless, if He did indeed come intending to tolerate and to preserve each man's idea regarding God rooted in him from of old.[7]

I have presented the conception of dialogue expressed by the philosophers of science not only for its own sake, but to illustrate a larger question: the impact of the philosophy of an era on ecumenical dialogue. In this first part, the topic of discussion was dialogue as such, and not its content. We have perhaps succeeded in establishing that philosophical conditioning cannot be excluded from an understanding of the nature of dialogue. We will now address an aspect of dialogue's content: namely, the Reformation's philosophical presuppositions regarding the relationship between God and man.

---

[7] Ibid., Book 3, ch. 12, no. 6.

PART II

The Philosophical Presuppositions of the Reformation

As MENTIONED in the introduction, the idea that the Reformation could have broken totally with all philosophical conditioning is untenable, especially since the Reformation paid no explicit attention to philosophy. For historical reasons, particularly Luther's personal antipathy toward the philosophy which was taught him, and the resolve to break with the immediate past which was a defining characteristic of the Reformation even to its very name, Protestantism has rarely taken note of its grounding in the philosophy which preceded it. Even later, when Protestant theologians became very solicitous to keep track of the philosophy of their times, the idea did not even cross their minds that some of their presuppositions might depend on an ancient Scholastic construction. Anxious to find the most favorable ground for dialogue, and themselves scarcely aware that their partners might be influenced by philosophical factors, Catholic theologians have seldom broached the question.

We will begin with a historical introduction of Luther's attitude toward philosophy, and then try to establish parallels with Calvin and contemporary Protestantism.

CHAPTER I

Luther and Philosophy

LUTHER WAS AN INVETERATE ENEMY of philosophy and its involvement in theology.[1] In 1509, the young student Martin Luther (aged twenty-six) was already writing to one of his friends about how tiresome philosophy was for him: "If you want to know my condition, I am well, thanks be to God, except that my study does me violence, especially that of philosophy, which from the beginning I would have gladly exchanged for theology."[2] This antipathy, which can be

---

[1] For a brief and clear presentation of the relationship between Luther and philosophy, see the classic work by Gerhard Ebeling, *Luther: Introduction à une réflexion théologique* (Geneva: Labor et Fides, 1981), 73–83; for the present-day state of the question, see Herbert Blöchle, *Luthers Stellung zum Heidentum im Spannungsfeld von Tradition, Humanismus und Reformation* (Frankfurt am Main: Peter Lang, 1995). We unfortunately became acquainted too late with a work which we cannot take into consideration here: Teodor Dieter, *Der junge Luther und Aristoteles: Eine historisch-systematische Untersuchung zum Verhältnis von Theologie und Philosophie* (Berlin: De Gruyter, 2001). I have expressed my thanks to this book in *Nova et Vetera*.

[2] "Quod si statum meum nosse desideres, bene habeo Dei gratia, nisi quod violentum est studium, maxime philosophiae, quam ego ab initio libentissime mutarim theologia . . ." Letter V, March 1509, to Johannes Braun (WA *Br* 1.17.40–43). Cf. also Letter 61, March 1518, to Spalatin (WA *Br* 1.150.17/–19) where Luther recalls his memories: "Ego sepius cum amicis disquisivi, Quidnam videretur nobis utilitatis accessisse ex tam anxiis studiis philosophie et Dialectice."

partially explained by the instruction he received in his youth, would often later be expressed in unequivocal terms. The personal motives for Luther's rejection of philosophy can be traced to the partial degeneration of Scholasticism, and the neglect or misuse of Scripture within the theology with which he was acquainted in youth. But the reality of this rejection remains, and its importance has not yet been fully weighed. Every reader of Luther knows that his blunt formulae need to be nuanced. He certainly does not consider his opposition to philosophy a motive which is central to his reforming action.[3] Moreover, he does not deny all utility to non-Christian thought. He accepts the value of the pagan authors insofar as they do not trespass on theological ground. Thus he can appreciate the pagan poets,[4] pagan mythology,[5] Roman law,[6] and the like on a profane level. As for the application of philosophy to theology, he sometimes sees it in a positive light, as long as it is restricted to the profane domain, or remains as an external aid to reading the Bible (for instance, in the case of logic[7] or grammar[8]). Fric-

---

[3] I have to agree with Georg Kretschmar, "La foi et l'éthique chez les réformateurs," in Académie Internationale des Sciences Religieuses, L'éthique: perspectives proposées par la foi, Jean-Louis Leuba, dir., Le point théologique 56 (Paris: Beauchesne; Louvain-la Neuve: Artel, 1993), 160 [here translated from French]: "It was certainly not in a struggle to liberate theology from philosophy that Luther became a reformer, any more than any of the other great reformers of the sixteenth century." The driving force of Luther's reforming activity is primarily spiritual rather than intellectual.

[4] Cf. Blöchle, Luthers Stellung, 77–79.

[5] Cf. ibid., 91–93.

[6] Cf. ibid., 106–8.

[7] Cf. ibid., 97–99.

[8] "1. Sacra theologia, etsi est doctrina divinitus inspirata, non tamen abhorret literis et vocibus tradi. 2. Inter omnes scientias humanitus inventas precipue est ad propagandam theologiam utilis grammatica. 3. Non ideo in Aristotele et eius philosophia studendum est, quia terminis eisdem quandoque sancti doctores utuntur" ("Conclusiones

tion arises, however, wherever pagan thought enters into theology's own domain. Characteristically, Luther rejects pagan cosmology in favor of the cosmology in Genesis:[9] although natural philosophy can be useful to theology (in order to understand the natural phenomena in the Bible), one must reject the path which leads to a cosmology that conflicts with the Bible's, and thence to natural theology.[10] The prospect of opposition between the Bible and certain philosophical positions is compounded by Luther's lack of confidence in philosophy's potential. He is familiar with the antagonism between Scholastic schools in the universities: in his own University of Wittenberg, the *via Thomae*, the *via Scoti*, and finally the nominalist *via moderna*, which he would represent at one point, were all taught.[11] He contrasts

---

quindecim tractantes, An libri philosophorum sint utiles aunt inutiles ad theologiam," WA 6.29; this text dates probably from 1519).

Luther elsewhere clarifies that philosophical dialectic is different from theological dialectic, because the meaning of words is different in Scripture: "Quomodo ergo, inquam, prodest Dialectica, cum, postquam accessero ad Theologiam, id vocabuli, quod in Dialectica sic significabat, cogar reiicere et aliam eis significationem accipere?" (L. 61, March 1518, to Spalatin, WA *Br* 1.150.25–28).

9   Luther's 1535–45 lectures on the Epistle to the Romans describe the creation of the world and conclude: "Ergo de causis istarum rerum nos Christiani aliter sentire debemus quam Philosophi, et si quaedem sunt supra captum nostrum (sicut ista hic de aquis supra coelos), ea potius sunt cum nostrae ignorantiae confessione credenda, quam aut impie credenda, aut arroganter pro nostro captu interpretanda. Oportet enim nos servare phrasin scripturae sanctae, et manere in verbis Spiritus sancti . . ." (WA 42.23.19–24).

10 Cf. the "Conclusiones quindecim tractantes, An libri philosophorum sint utiles aut inutiles ad theologiam," probably composed in 1519: "9. Philosophia de motu infinito, principiis rerum iuxta Aristotelem, nihil prodest ad theologiam. . . . 11. Philosophia de naturis et proprietatibus rerum . . . utilis est ad sacram theologiam" (WA 6.29).

11 Cf. D. R. Janz, "Thomas Aquinas, Martin Luther, and the Origins of the Protestant Reformation," *Medieval Studies* 12 (1991): 75: "Trained at Erfurt in the via moderna, Luther began his theological

the certainty of Revelation with the impossibility of consensus among philosophers: Thomists, Albertists, Scotists, and
Moderns tear each other apart, and their kingdom is divided
against itself.[12] If he happens to have a positive opinion of
Plato[13] (so much so that he risks being influenced by Plato's
dualism[14]), his opposition to philosophy becomes especially

---

career as an accamist. At the fledging University of Wittenberg, only
the via Thomae and the via Scoti were taught until 1507 when one
of Luther's teachers, Jodocus Trutvetter, was hired to represent the
via moderna there. . . . In 1510 Trutvetter returned to Erfurt and in
the following year Luther was appointed to represent the via moderna in Wittenberg. He was thus the second appointment in the via
moderna to a faculty heavily dominated by the via antiqua."

[12] "Vere enim sumus seducti per Aristotelem et commenta eius, atque si
aliud non esset, hoc unum satis erat argumentum, quod tot sectae et
capita sint in ista bestia gentili, simili Hydrae in Lerna: nam ibi sunt
Thomistae, Scotistae, Albertistae, Moderni, et factus est quadriceps
Aristoteles et regnum in seipsum divisum, et mirum quod non desoletur, sed prope est ut desoletur. Quomodo ergo potest fieri, ut veri-
tas sit in tanta opinionum confusione? cum enim sint contrariae,
necesse est ut et falsae" (WA 1.509.11–17, dating from 1518). "Quin
et seipsos inter sese mordent et consumunt, Thomistae, Scotistate,
Moderni, acuuntque invicem non quosvis, sed leonum dentes" (WA
7.739.1–2, dating from 1521). The *Resolutiones disputationum de
indulgentiarum virtute* (concl. LVIII, WA 1.611–612, LW 31, 222), a
commentary on the 95 Theses composed in 1518, indulges in
polemic against the Aristotelians: "for more than 300 years now,
many universities, and many of the sharpest minds in them, have
labored with persistent industry to comprehend Aristotle alone. Yet
they not only do not understand Aristotle after all this effort but even
disseminate error and a false understanding of him throughout
almost the whole church. And even if they should understand him,
they would have attained no extraordinary wisdom thereby, particularly not from the Aristotelian books with which they are most familiar. According to his own testimony in the fourth chapter of book
twenty by Aulus Gellius, and according to the testimony of Gregory
Nazianzen in his *Sermon against the Arians,* Aristotle is discovered to
be nothing more than a mere sophist and a bandier of words."

[13] Cf. Théobald Süss, *Luther,* Philosophes (Paris: Presses Universitaires
de France, 1969), 15–20, 65, 68–72.

[14] Cf. ibid., 60–61. This influence concerns the relationship between
the interior and the exterior man.

fierce when he speaks of the "most impious Aristotle, public enemy or *ex professo* of truth, the least of whose sentences are adversaries of Christ,"[15] that "devastator of the holy doctrine," whose teachings Thomas disseminated,[16] that "blind pagan."[17] The works of Aristotle were given to man by the devil after he snatched the Bible from them.[18] The "king of philosophers" and "triple Cerberus" is the Angel of the Abyss, and if Scripture does not explicitly specify his identity, it is because the Stagyrite's name is not even worthy to be mentioned in the sacred text.[19] Luther may have acquired his anti-Aristotelian prejudices from his theological studies.[20] In May 1518, before his meeting with Cajetan, Luther states his preference for Plato[21] or Anaxagoras.[22]

---

15 "ut impiissimi Aristotelis, publici veritatis vel ex professo hostis, sententias quantumlibet Christo adversarias" (WA 6,186, II.14–15, 1520).

16 "Thomas multa haeretica scripsit et autor est regnantis Aristotelis, vastatoris piae doctrinae" (WA 8,127, II.19–20, 1521).

17 "der blinde Heide Aristoteles" (WA 10,1.2, 116, I.11, 1522).

18 Cf. WA 4,554, 18, II.31–38 (1516): the devil takes the Bible from Christians and gives them in its place the "maledicta figmenta Aristotelica."

19 "Et habebant super se regem, angelum Abyssi, cui nomen hebraice Abbadon (cf. Rev 9:11). . . . Quem ergo? Lumen illud naturae, scilicet Aristotelem, qui vere ἀπολλυων id est, perdens et vastator Ecclesiae, in universitatibus regnat. Neque enim dignus erat nominari in sacris literis suo nomine. Diximus enim, Angelum significare doctorem in Ecclesia. Et certum est, Aristotelem mortuum et damnatum esse doctorem hodie omnium universitatum magis quam Christum. Quia autoritate et studio Thomae elevatus regnat, resuscitans liberum arbitrium, docens virtutes morales et philosophiam naturalem, et triceps scilicet Cerberus, immo tricorpor Gerion" (WA 7,739, II.19–30, 1521).

20 Cf. Marc Lienhard, Introduction to *Oeuvres*, vol. 1, by Martin Luther, Bibliothèque de la Pléiade (Paris: Gallimard, 1999), xvii.

21 Cf. Luther, *Heidelberg Disputation* (May 1518), thesis 36, LW 31, 42: *"Aristotle wrongly finds fault with and derides the ideas of Plato, which actually are better than his own."*

22 Cf. ibid., thesis 39, LW 31, 42: *"If Anaxagoras posited infinity as to form, as it seems he did, he was the best of the philosophers, even if Aristotle was unwilling to acknowledge this."*

The motives for such hostility are not only philosophical: Aristotle is often mentioned in connection with Thomas, and Luther was hostile to Thomists for many reasons, which included the antagonism between the Augustinians and Dominicans.[23]

Besides these context-based factors, Luther is also directly opposed to Aristotle's philosophy itself and to its use in theology: beginning in 1517, he rejects both Aristotle's ethics, which assert that works can lead to beatitude, and the notion that one must necessarily go through Aristotle to become a theologian.[24] He wants theology to recover its independence and dignity through liberation from Aristotle, so that priority can be given to reading Scripture by means of the "hermeneutic key," that is, the experience of Christ as Savior. Even before the conventional beginning of the Reformation, Luther tends to reject the philosophy with which he is familiar, partly in order to promote the primacy of faith in Christ the Savior:

> Indeed I for my part believe that I owe to the Lord this
> duty of speaking out against philosophy and of persuading
> men to heed Holy Scripture. For perhaps if another man
> who has not seen these things, did this, he might be afraid

---

[23] See for instance a few pages on this topic in Morerod, *Cajetan et Luther en 1518: Edition, traduction et commentaire des opuscules d'Augsbourg de Cajetan,* Cahiers Oecuméniques 26 (Fribourg, Switzerland: Éditions Universitaires, 1994), vol. 1, pp. 38–41.

[24] Cf. his *Disputation against Scholastic Theology* from the end of August, 1517, LW 31, 12: "41. Virtually the entire *Ethics* of Aristotle is the worst enemy of grace. This in opposition to the scholastics. 42. It is an error to maintain that Aristotle's statement concerning happiness does not contradict Catholic doctrine. This in opposition to the doctrine on morals. 43. It is an error to say that no man can become a theologian without Aristotle. This in opposition to common opinion. 44. Indeed, no one can become a theologian unless he becomes one without Aristotle. (. . .) 50. Briefly, the whole Aristotle is to theology as darkness is to light. This in opposition to the scholastics."

or he might not be believed. But I have been worn out by
these studies for many years now, and having experienced
and heard many things over and over again, I have come to
see that it is the study of vanity and perdition. Therefore I
warn you all as earnestly as I can that you finish these studies quickly and let it be your only concern not to establish
and defend them but treat them as we do when we learn
worthless skills to destroy them and study errors to refute
them. Thus we study also these things to get rid of them,
or at least, just to learn the method of speaking of those
people with whom we must carry on some discourse. For it
is high time that we undertake new studies and learn Jesus
Christ, "and Him crucified" (1 Cor. 2:2).[25]

Luther's reticence toward Scholasticism can be explained
not only by his rejection of philosophy, but also by his rejection of Scholastic theology, permeated as it was with Aristotle. Luther, however, had come to know Scholasticism primarily through reading Gabriel Biel[26] (1408–95), whose
writings guided his studies[27] and whom, Melanchthon
asserts, he could still quote by heart at the end of his life.[28]
Biel's influence on Luther is well known, at least since the

---

[25] Luther, *Lectures on Romans* (ca. 1516), LW 25, 361.

[26] For a short biography, see Franz-Josef Burkard, "Gabriel Biel," in
Lexikon für Theologie und Kirche (Freiburg: Herder, 1994), vol. 2,
col. 437. For a more detailed biography, with a short presentation of
works, see Werner Dettloff, "Gabriel Biel," in *Theologische Realenzyklopädie*, (Berlin: W. de Gruyter, 1980), vol. 6, pp. 488–91; John
L. Farthing, "Gabriel Biel," in *Routledge Encyclopedia of Philosophy*
(London: Routledge, 1998), 769–72.

[27] Cf. Otto Hermann Pesch, *Hinführung zu Luther* (Mainz: Matthias-
Grünewald-Verlag, 1982), 72: "Sein wichtigstes Lehrbuch ist der
Sentenzenkommentar des Gabriel Biels (ca. 1410–1495), das soge-
nannte 'Collectorium.' "

[28] Cf. John L. Farthing, *Thomas Aquinas and Gabriel Biel: Interpretation of St. Thomas Aquinas in German Nominalism on the Eve of the
Reformation,* Duke Monographs in Medieval and Renaissance Studies 9 (London: Duke University Press, 1998), 100.

works of Leif Grane[29] and Heiko Augustinus Oberman.[30] Biel was an "open" nominalist and often quoted Thomas Aquinas favorably;[31] consequently, Luther assumed that he had had access to Thomas's thought, whereas he did not actually know Thomas directly[32] (it should also be noted that some Thomists were not very faithful to St. Thomas on topics such as merit[33]). From 1517 on, Luther was clearly reacting against Biel, notably with respect to free will, the importance of which we will discuss later:

> 6. It is false to state that the will can by nature conform to correct precept. This is said in opposition to Scotus and Gabriel. (. . .) 10. One must concede that the will is not free to strive toward whatever is declared good. This in opposition to Scotus and Gabriel[34]

What then does Biel say about free will? First of all, he asserts that without free will, morality does not exist: "the power to sin does not exist without free will, since nothing lacking free

---

[29] Cf. Leif Grane, *Contra Gabrielem: Luthers Auseinandersetzung mit Gabriel Biel in der Disputatio contra scholasticam theologiam 1517,* Acta theologica danica 4 (Kopenhagen: Gyldendal, 1962).

[30] Cf. Heiko Augustinus Oberman, *The Harvest of Medieval Theology: Gabriel Biel and Late Medieval Nominalism,* rev. ed. (Grand Rapids: Eerdmans, 1967).

[31] For the relationship of Biel with St. Thomas, cf. Farthing, *Thomas Aquinas and Gabriel Biel.*

[32] Cf. Otto Hermann Pesch, *Thomas d'Aquin: Grandeur et limites de la théologie médiévale,* Cogitatio Fidei 177 (Paris: Cerf, 1994), 17 [here translated from French]: "Luther, who is barely encumbered by real knowledge of Aquinas, and not at all by the personal reading of his works . . ."

[33] Cf. Otto Hermann Pesch, *Die Theologie der Rechtfertigung bei Martin Luther und Thomas von Aquin: Versuch eines systematisch-theologischen Dialogs,* Walberberger Studien 4 (Mainz: Matthias-Grünewald-Verlag, 1967), 788.

[34] Luther, *Disputation against Scholastic Theology,* no. 6 and 10, LW 31, 9–10.

will can sin."[35] He admits, however, that the only proof he can furnish for the existence of free will is experience: "Can it be sufficiently proven that the will is free? We reply to this briefly, following Ockham [. . .] and Gregory da Rimini [. . .] that it is evident from experience that the will is free by a contingent freedom, and accordingly, this 'cannot be proven by anything more evident.'"[36] Yet despite its uncertainty, Biel invokes free will in his theology of merit, which is problematic, to say the least: "as to its essence, the meritorious act . . . proceeds from the will as from its first or principal cause, and from grace as from its secondary or less principal cause."[37] He then hastens to add that merit exists only when God accepts an act as meritorious,[38] giving the impression

---

35 "Respondetur quod posse peccare non est sine libero arbitrio, quia nihil carens arbitrio potest peccare" (Gabriel Biel, *Collectorium circa quattuor libros sententiarum* [hereafter CCQLS], Auspiciis H. Rückert, ed. W. Werbeck and U. Hofmann, 5 vol. [Tübingen: J. C. B. Mohr, 1973–77] [index, 1992]; here L. II, dist. 25, quaestio unica, art. 1, resp., vol. 2, p. 484). Cf. also CCQLS, L.II, dist. 25, quaestio unica, art. 3, dubium 2, vol. 2, p. 492: "Quia, si homo nihil per liberum arbitrium ageret' vel omitteret, 'frustra esset omnes humanum consilium, ut deducit *Damascenus* II cap. 28. 'Nullus' etiam 'pro suis actibus merebitur praemium vel poenam, ut ostendit *Augustinus* II De libero arbitrio cap. 2.' Sic etiam 'divina pracepta homini non prodessent,' si non libere servando perveniret ad praemium."

36 "Secundo dubitatur: 'Utrum possit sufficienter probari, quod voluntas sit libera.' Ad hoc breviter respondetur secundum Occam Quodlibeto I q. 16 et Gregorium de Arimino distinctione praesenti, quod voluntatem esse liberam libertate contingentiae est evidens per experientiam, et ideo 'non potest per aliquid evidentius demonstrari'" (CCQLS, L. II, dist. 25, quaestio unica, art. 3, dubium 2, vol. 2, p. 491).

37 "Actus ergo meritorius quantum ad substantiam eius, intensionem et moralem rectitudinem est a voluntate tamquam a causa prima sive principali et a gratia tamquam a causa secunda sive minus principali; qualis est generaliter habitus respectu potentiae" (CCQLS, L. II, dist. 27, quaestio unica, art. 3, dubium 2, vol. 2, p. 520). Note though that here he is expressing a *dubium*.

38 "Quantum vero ad rationem meriti non ita. Nam ratio meriti principalissime convenit actui ex libera acceptatione divina. Nam illa

that a meritorious act really proceeds primarily from us, and that God's role is limited to subsequent ratification of our acts. Luther would adopt the diametrically opposite position: "On the part of man, however, nothing precedes grace except indisposition and even rebellion against grace."[39] Biel adds another consideration, concerning the love of God above all things:

> Even if in the case considered by this question, sin is not avoided without grace . . . nevertheless, this does not derive "absolutely from the impotence of our free will" [Scotus]— one could in fact choose an act of love of God above all things by one's own natural powers, even if grace were not infused—but from the generosity of God, who gives grace to the free will which is in some way well disposed.[40]

Biel gives the impression of asserting that although grace is not really necessary, it is generously given by God even in the most elevated act possible, that of loving God above all else.[41] Luther would later react violently against these propositions; in fact, one of the foundational elements of his entire theology is the absolute rejection of merit. He is

---

existente, omnibus aliis semotis, actus est meritorius, ut I dist. 17 patuit; illa non existente, omnibus aliis positis, non est meritorius" (Ibid.).

[39] Luther, *Disputation against Scholastic Theology,* no. 30, LW 31, 11.

[40] "licet in casu dubii non cavetur peccatum sine gratia, quia actus dilectionis Dei super omnia est dispositio ultimata et sufficiens de congruo ad gratiae infusionem, qua existente simul gratia infunditur, hoc tamen non est 'propter impotentiam liberi arbitrii absolute'—posset enim actum dilectionis Dei super omnia elicere ex suius naturalibus, etiam si gratia non infunderetur—sed ex liberalitate Dei gratiam liberaliter infundentis libero arbitrio aliqualiter bene disposito" (CCQLS, L. II, dist. 28, quaestio unica, art. 3, dubium 1, vol. II, pp. 539–40).

[41] Here too, Biel certainly expresses a dubium, a question which needs clarification. But, in his doubt, following Scotus, he tends toward a solution which could not satisfy Luther.

right to say that man is not prior to grace, because God has
the supreme initiative in our salvation. But he goes to the
opposite extreme, affirming that "[w]hen it has been
proved that salvation is beyond our own powers and
devices, and depends on the work of God alone (. . .), does
it not follow that when God is not present and at work in
us everything we do is evil and we necessarily do what is of
no avail for salvation?"[42] or again that "[i]t cannot be
denied that love is superfluous if man is by nature able to
do an act of friendship. In opposition to Gabriel."[43] The
opposition which he generally places between God and the
'natural' man is also manifested in the following statement:
"One ought rather to conclude: since erring man is able to
love the creature it is impossible for him to love God."[44]

Luther's criticism of philosophy, then, is essentially a
reaction against Scholasticism, for reasons which are theological, not philosophical. Nevertheless, every reaction
tends to be based, at least in part, on the position it is
attacking. Thus it is not unlikely that Luther retained certain presuppositions from his adversaries, especially since
they were responsible for his formation.

Finally, Luther has a genius for communication. One
reason for his success is his unusual capacity for perceiving
the culture of his time. Thus he perceived the unfolding of
a philosophical movement, without even calling it philosophical. Gabriella Cotta's summary provides a fitting conclusion to our brief presentation of Luther's attitude toward
philosophy:

> I believe that a thinker like Luther, certainly not stripped of
> philosophical knowledge, but doubtless a fierce critic of the

---

42 Luther, *The Bondage of the Will*, LW 33, 64.
43 Luther, *Disputation against Scholastic Theology*, no. 92, LW 31, 15.
44 Luther, *Disputation against Scholastic Theology*, no. 16, LW 31, 10.

then-dominant—and, in his opinion ruinous—orientation
of this discipline, whose excessive claims he challenged in
every opportunity, succeeded in conceiving and revealing,
probably beyond his own intention, the principal themes of
the speculative revolution of his own times. That is why, in
my opinion, if one wishes to understand Luther fully, one
cannot totally disregard the constant philosophical implications of his thought, even less than one can ignore the
unmistakably important historical and biographical facts
which are almost always mentioned in the works dedicated
to him. It is precisely on account of his formidable capacity
for manipulating, divulging, and leading such themes to
their fulfilment, that Luther's work was able to cause such
turmoil in all domains: social, political, cultural—besides,
of course, the religious sphere.[45]

---

[45] "Ritengo perciò che proprio un pensatore como Lutero, non certo
digiuno di conoscenze filosofiche, ma certamente feroce critico del-
l'impostazione ancora dominante—e a suo avviso rovinosa—di tale
disciplina, di cui non perdeva occasione di rilevare le eccesive pretese,
sia riuscito a concepire e divulgare—probabilmente al di là delle sui
intenzioni—i temi principali della rivoluzione speculativa del suo
tempo. A mio avviso, perciò, volendo capire Lutero pienamente, non
si può prescindere, ben più che dai pur importantissimi dati storici e
biografici, quasi sempre presenti nelle opere a lui dedicate, dalle continue implicazioni filosofiche del suo pensiero. È proprio in ragione
della sua formidabile capacità di portare a compimento, veicolare e
divulgare tali temi, che l'opera di Lutero, infatti, ha potuto produrre
rivolgimenti in ogni ambito: sociale, politico, culturale—oltre che,
naturalmente, religioso" (Cotta, *La nascita dell'individualismo politico:
Lutero e la politica della modernità* [Bologna: Il Mulino, 2002], 9–10).

CHAPTER 2

Cajetan's Critique of
Luther on Causality

IT IS OFTEN THOUGHT that the problem with Luther's ecclesiology is his denial of the divine institution of Church structures. If the controversy is presented in these terms, it gives rise to an exegetical and historical study in which real agreement cannot be obtained. A deeper level of analysis is necessary. Luther's ecclesiology depends on his theology of justification: this connection is generally easy to see. I suggest that we dig even deeper, to unearth the presuppositions of the Lutheran doctrine of justification. This is not an attempt to reduce the theology of justification to a philosophical doctrine, neglecting the impact of Luther's personal history. Rather, the question here relates to the precise manner of explaining justification. Why does Luther explain justification the way he does, and not as the Council of Trent does, for instance? I am convinced that the presupposition which underlies the doctrine of justification as Luther expresses it is in fact a philosophical theory of causality. This is what Cajetan pointed out as early as 1518.

Cajetan and Luther

The debate on justification centers on the relationship between divine and human action. This issue emerges in the debate between Luther and one of his first "opponents," the Thomist Cajetan.[1] Thomas Aquinas and Duns Scotus appear in the background. We will begin with an exposition of what I consider to be the central point of their debate. We will then examine the extent of this debate's contemporary relevance.

In October 1518, Luther appeared before Cardinal Cajetan (1469–1534), the papal legate in Augsburg. This appearance, which was judiciary, not theological, was obtained by Luther's protector, the elector Frederick of Saxony, in an attempt to prevent the proceedings from taking place in Rome. To prepare himself personally for the confrontation, Cajetan studied those few texts from Luther's pen which he could find (Luther was only at the beginning of his theological production and was still relatively unknown),[2] and he assembled his thoughts on these works into fifteen opuscula. I will summarize briefly and with a

---

[1] For the meeting between Cajetan and Luther, see the bibliography in Charles Morerod, *Cajetan et Luther en 1518*. Let us mention in particular the two authors who have contributed to the rediscovery of this encounter: Gerhard Hennig, *Cajetan und Luthers: Ein historischer Beitrag zur Begegnung von Thomismus und Reformation*, "Arbeiten zur Theologie," 2nd ed., vol. 7 (Stuttgart: Calwer Verlag, 1966); Jared Wicks, *Cajetan Responds: A Reader in Reformation Controversy* (Washington, D.C.: Catholic University of America Press, 1978), and *Cajetan und die Anfänge der Reformation*, Katholisches Leben und Kämpfen im Zeitalter der Glaubensspaltung, Vereinsschriften der Gesselschaft zur Herausgabe des Corpus Catholicorum 43 (aus dem englischen Manuskript übersetzt von Barbara Hallensleben), (Münster: Aschendorff, 1983). A more recent discussion specifically focusing on Cajetan's meeting with Luther, which is historically accurate although sparsely developed theologically and lacking any reference to the question of philosophy, can be found in Anthony Levi, *Renaissance and Reformation: The Intellectual Genesis* (London: Yale University Press, 2002), 277–84.

[2] The texts on which Cajetan based his evaluation are the following: First, the *Resolutiones disputationum de indulgentiarum virtute*, which Luther sent on May 30, 1518, to his superior Johann von Staupitz, so that the latter could forward them to Pope Leo X, to whom they were dedicated (text and introduction: WA 1, pp. 522–628). These

limited bibliography the points which I have already developed elsewhere, and which I wish to situate in a broader context than that of the beginning of the sixteenth century.[3]

In reading these opuscula, composed at a time when the breadth of the nascent phenomenon was not yet evident, we must keep in mind not so much our subsequent knowledge of Luther and the Reformation (an anachronism to which many commentators on this famous encounter have succumbed), but primarily Cajetan's intellectual history as a Thomist theologian who had been engaged for some thirty years in the struggle against Scotism. In the years which followed, Cajetan would devote other works to the Reformation, this time with clearer insight into the nature of the movement which had begun to divide Christianity.

Up to that point, Cajetan's theological debates had pitted him against Scotism. In reading Luther's arguments, he recognized a Scotist flavor of which Luther himself, not to mention the majority of later readers concentrating on the main themes of the Reformation, was unaware. My intent here is not to analyze Scotus, much less to see him as a proto-Reformer or as the absolute historical originator of the themes which would become "Protestant," and the like. Rather, I am seeking only to point out how Luther was impacted by a certain kind of thinking which he had imbibed indirectly and

---

Resolutiones developed the theses on indulgences which were publicly displayed or sent toward the beginning of November 1517 and which are considered the foundational act of the Reformation. This is the most significant text. Second, the *Sermo de penitentia* (WA 1, pp. 317–24), given before Easter 1518, which is closely related to a *Sermon von Ablass und Gnade* preceding it by a few months (WA 1, pp. 239–46). Third, a *sermo de virtute excommunicationis* (WA 1, pp. 634–43), given c. May 15th of the same year and revised at the end of August 1518, which would earn Luther a denunciation to the Pope from Emperor Maximilian I.

3 For more detailed information, see Morerod, *Cajetan et Luther en 1518*. This work includes citations from Cajetan's opuscula.

which continued to influence him unconsciously. Cajetan saw the connection between the two theologians.

Cajetan's Choice of Arguments in his Study of Luther

What positions does Luther defend in the works which Cajetan was able to read before their encounter? His arguments relate to indulgences, Purgatory (whose existence Luther does not deny at the moment, but which he discusses in connection with indulgences), the sacrament of Penance, and excommunication. Cajetan chose these themes not out of personal interest, but because he found them in Luther's writings. They would serve as the starting point from which Cajetan would be able to unveil the Augustinian's theological presuppositions.

Some of Luther's arguments, developed in his Ninety-Five Theses of 1517 and in the 1518 commentary on the theses (which Cajetan would read), relate to abuses crying for reform. The Dominican theologian wasted no time on such arguments: he preferred to go straight to the theological heart of the matter, at the risk of underestimating the impact of practical factors. We will therefore investigate these theological aspects, without thereby negating the importance of the historical issues involved.

In order to understand how Cajetan perceived the theological issues, we should introduce them with reference to a prior debate, in which Thomists and Scotists were pitted against each other on the question of analogy and univocity.

Analogy for Thomas, Univocity for Scotus

Luther's background, theological heritage, and implicit philosophy were shaped by the dispute over the analogy or univocity of being. In order to illuminate Luther's position, as well as his debate with Cajetan, we must briefly sketch the debate between the positions of St. Thomas Aquinas and Bl. Duns Scotus (whose teaching Luther imbibed through Biel rather than directly from the original, unaware of its source, since Biel himself was not explicitly a Scotist).

This debate begins as an exploration of the possibility of speaking about God, and ends with each side supporting a different understanding of God's Being and of his relationship to us.

St. Thomas is aware that our language about God is necessarily limited, to the point of saying: "because we cannot know what God is, but rather what He is not, we have no means for considering how God is, but rather how He is not."[4] Nevertheless, Revelation encourages him to believe that we can speak of God.[5]

For him, the primary rule of our language about God is that "no name is predicated univocally of God and of creatures. Neither, on the other hand, are names applied to God and creatures in a purely equivocal sense. . . . Therefore it must be said that these names are said of God and creatures in an analogous sense, i.e. according to proportion."[6] This concept of analogy has had varying interpretations in the history of theology, even among St. Thomas's commentators.[7] I will endeavor to present here a typical definition, aiming for essentials and referring only to the main conditions of our

---

[4] Ia, q. 3, Prologue.

[5] I am thinking not only of discourse about God explicitly founded on Revelation, but also of the fact that some biblical texts explicitly presuppose a certain "natural theology." For an example of the revival of such a viewpoint among Protestant theologians, cf. James Barr, *Biblical Faith and Natural Theology* (New York: Oxford University Press, Clarendon Paperbacks, 1993).

[6] Ia, q. 13, a. 5.

[7] Cf. the overview given by Bernard Montagnes, *La doctrine de l'analogie de l'être d'après saint Thomas d'Aquin*, vol. 6 of *Philosophes médiévaux* (Louvain: Publications universitaires; Paris: Éd. Béatrice-Nauwelaerts, 1963).

language about God. When we say that God is good (or that he is true, or simply that he is), we are trying to express that there is a common ground between the meaning of "good" when we speak of God and of creatures. Nevertheless, "one there is who is good" (Mt 19:17 RSV): in the community of goodness between God and us, God alone infinitely realizes what we can only realize in a limited way. And this is possible because we have been created by God and retain the imprint, even the likeness, of our Creator. In analogical discourse, we must remember that the difference between God and us is such that negating common elements is in itself more accurate than affirming them, but does not absolutely preclude the latter. And in our affirmations, we retain only the eminent perfection of the perfections which we express, not the mixed realization which we observe in ourselves. In other words, the first who is good, is God; in another use of analogy, one could say that the first who is Father, is God.[8] Let us not make God in our own image under pretext of using our own words, for it is we who are in his image.

The *Catechism of the Catholic Church* summarizes this position:

> Since our knowledge of God is limited, our language about him is equally so. We can name God only by taking creatures as our starting point, and in accordance with our limited human ways of knowing and thinking.
>
> All creatures bear a certain resemblance to God, most especially man created in the image and likeness of God. . . .
>
> God transcends all creatures. We must therefore continually purify our language of everything in it that is limited, imagebound or imperfect. . . .

---

8 Cf. the rules for using analogy, for example in Charles Journet, *Connaissance et inconnaissance de Dieu* (Fribourg: Librairie de l'Université, 1943), 21–26; or Jean-Hervé Nicolas, *Dieu connu comme inconnu* (Paris: Desclée de Brouwer, 1966), 142–48.

> Admittedly, in speaking about God like this, our language is using human modes of expression; nevertheless it does really attain to God himself, though unable to express him in his infinite simplicity.[9]

More recently, the encyclical *Fides et Ratio* expressed the same idea:

> Faith clearly presupposes that human language is capable of expressing divine and transcendent reality in a universal way—analogically, it is true, but no less meaningfully for that. Were this not so, the word of God, which is always a divine word in human language, would not be capable of saying anything about God.[10]

Scotus denied St. Thomas's view on this point, since he felt that it posed an insuperable obstacle to all discourse about God. His goal is clearly the same as Thomas's: namely, to make discourse about God possible. Nevertheless, Scotus perceives analogous concepts as being too different (corresponding more to what Thomas called equivocal concepts). From this he deduces that if discourse about God is to be possible, we should be able to engage in it using our own concepts in their unique and thus comprehensible sense. And for him, this involves speaking of God quidditatively, that is, saying what God is. He expresses this opinion in the following text:

> I say, first, that one can naturally have not only a concept in which God is conceived accidentally, for instance in some attribute, but also a certain concept in which God is conceived in himself and quidditatively. . . . I say, second, that

---

9 *Catechism of the Catholic Church*, 2nd ed., (Vatican City: Libreria Editrice Vaticana for the United States Conference of Catholic Bishops, 1997), para. 40-43.

10 John Paul II, encyclical letter *Fides et Ratio* (September 14, 1998), no. 84.

God is not conceived only in a concept analogous to the
concept of the creature, namely in a concept which might be
altogether different from that which is spoken of the creature, but in a concept which is univocal to him [God] and to
the creature. And so that no one will dispute about the word
"univocation," I call univocal a concept which is one in such
a manner that its unity suffices for contradiction when one
affirms or negates it with respect to the same object.[11]

This dispute is partially a misunderstanding, which Bernardino Bonansea summarizes best:

Although Thomas and Scotus are substantially in agreement in recognizing the diverse modes of predicating the
perfections of God which Pseudo-Dionysius indicates,
Thomas founds such a predication on the doctrine of analogy, Scotus on that of univocity. The two theories are not
necessarily contrary one to the other, because univocity
does not have the same meaning for both Doctors.[12]

Luther never became involved in this controversy. He was
content to comment on Scripture, rejecting the distinctions

---

[11] "Dico ergo primo quod non tantum haberi potest conceptus natu-
raliter in quo quasi per accidens concipitur Deus, puta in aliquod
attributo, sed etiam aliquis conceptus in quo per se et quidditative
concipiatur Deus. . . . Secundo dico quod non tantum in conceptu
analogo conceptui creaturae concipitur Deus, scilicet qui omnino sit
alius ab illo qui de creatura dicitur, sed in conceptu aliquo univoco sibi
et creaturae. Et ne fiat contentio de nomine univocationis, univocum
conceptum dico qui ita est unus quod ejus unitas sufficit ad contradic-
tionem affirmando et negando ipsum de eodem." (Duns Scotus,
Ordinatio I, dist. III, pars I, q. 1, in *Opera omnia*, vol. 3, 16–18).

[12] "Benchè Tommaso e Scoto siano sostanzialmente d'accordo nell'am-
mettere i vari modi di predicazione delle perfezioni di Dio indicate
dallo Pseudo-Dionigi, Tommaso fonda tale predicazione sulla dott-
rina dell'analogia, Scoto su quella dell'univocità. Le due teorie non
sono necessariamente contrarie l'una all'altra, perché l'univocità non
ha lo stesso significato per i due Dottori. Infatti per Scoto, univocità
significa identità di termine, concetto e realtà specifica o modalità a

of the Subtle Doctor along with those of the Angelic Doctor. Hence it is not surprising that this Scholastic debate has never been mentioned in discussions of Luther. It would be beneficial, however, to take it into consideration on account of its consequences. Each of the positions of these two doctors has its own particular dynamic, which primarily affects its conception of the being of God.

St. Thomas's position does not isolate language from being, even in discourse about God. We can speak of God not only in virtue of the kinship between our experience-based concepts and the concepts applied to God, but also because of a kinship of being resulting from the fact that God is the cause of our being. The grasp of what the levels of being can have in common, and how they differ, has an immediate impact on language.

The Thomist vision of analogy has a major consequence for understanding the relationship between God and us: namely, one and the same action can be accomplished entirely by God at his level, and by us at ours.

The Relation Between God and his Creatures as Causes

How then does St. Thomas understand the relationship between God's causality and the causality of creatures? It is evident how this question is related to Luther's question regarding the status of human works with respect to divine action. With the help of St. Thomas, Luther's question can be situated in its broader context.

---

cui il termine viene applicato, ma non identità degli esseri coinvolti presi nella loro completa realtà metafisica. È così che egli può parlare di ente come termine univoco che si applica a Dio e alle creature, anche se Dio è un Ente infinito e le creature sono enti finiti e variamente limitati" (Bernardino Bonansea, *L'uomo e Dio nel pensiero de Duns Scoto* [Milan: Jaca Book, 1991], 118–19).

In the relationship between higher and lower causes, we are confronted with two parallel scenarios. The first clearly pertains to God and his creature. In this case, we speak of first cause (God) and secondary cause (creature). The second scenario is that of principal cause versus instrumental cause. If God alone can be the first cause, he is not the only one who can be a principal cause. Creatures can be principal causes, which happens whenever we use some sort of instrument.

The terms can be defined as follows:[13] God is the first cause, that is, the sole universal cause. The difference between the first cause and the second cause is that the first cause is essentially in act and encompasses the very depths of being, while the second cause can only initiate ripples in being (thus it cannot create), and acts only insofar as it is moved by the first cause. Therefore, the action of a second cause is also—indeed primarily—the action of the first cause.

A similar relationship exists between the more important cause, called the principal cause, and the cause which it employs, called the instrumental cause:

> If we consider the agent in its relations with other higher or lower causes, we can make another distinction, between the principal cause and the instrumental cause. The first acts by its own activity and on its own behalf, like the painter; the second acts on behalf of another, like the paintbrush. . . . Second causes are always instrumental in

---

[13] St. Thomas constantly makes use of the concepts of first and second cause. Cf. the following summaries: A. Chollet, "Cause," in *Dictionnaire de Théologie Catholique* (Paris, 1910), vol. 2.2, esp. col. 2024–26); A. D. Sertillanges, appendix "Prédestination," in St. Thomas Aquinas, *Somme théologique,* La Revue des Jeunes ed., vol. 3 (Paris: Desclée; Rome: Tournai, 1926), 321–26; J.-H. Nicolas, "L'origine première des choses," *Revue Thomiste* [hereafter *RT*] 91 (1991): esp. 195–99.

relation to the first cause. . . . In relation to lower agents, they can be, and are, principal second causes.[14]

Our relation to God can therefore be illustrated by our relation to a paintbrush: the paintbrush does nothing without us, but we agree to use a paintbrush (the difference being that we need a paintbrush in order to paint, while God can do without us).

There is certainly a difference between first and second causes on the one hand, and principal and instrumental causes on the other; but what matters here is the kind of relationship which exists between the supreme cause and the cause which is subordinated to it.[15] The same goes for the relationship between God as first cause or principal cause and man as second cause or instrumental cause: in both cases, the two causes produce the same effect, one in subordination to the other, and not two different effects, two different parts of the effect, or two chronologically successive stages of the effect.

Thomas asks whether it is necessary to predicate both natural causes and divine causality, whenever one single cause suffices to produce an effect. And he replies that "it is not

---

14 "On distingue encore, si l'on considère l'agent dans ses rapports avec les autres causes supérieures ou inférieures, la cause principale et la cause instrumentale. La première agit par sa propre activité et pour son compte, comme le peintre, la seconde agit pour le compte d'un autre, comme le pinceau . . . Les causes secondes sont toujours instrumentales par rapport à la cause première. . . . Par rapport à des agents inférieurs, elles peuvent être et elles sont des causes secondes principales" (Chollet, "Cause," col. 2025–26).

15 Nevertheless, this difference should be kept in mind. Cajetan attacks Durandus of Saint-Pourçain, for whom all second causes are instrumental causes of God: the Thomist retorts that in that case, every natural action would be the action of God (cf. *In Summ. Theol.*, Ia, q. 45, a. 5, no. XIV). Durand's position would thus amount to eliminating the significance of the whole world. This tendency is not off-topic when speaking of Luther.

inappropriate for the same effect to be produced by a lower agent and God; by both immediately, though in different ways."[16] If God wants to use an instrument, he can certainly do so, without being thereby prevented from accomplishing the entirety of the action himself. Cardinal Journet illustrates this theory by a simple example. Who makes a rose—God, or the rosebush? The rose is at once and without any competition the effect of the rosebush as second cause, and of God as first cause. And thus it happens that God makes a rose through the rosebush, and not without it.[17]

Nevertheless, one may ask what the role of the created cause is. Is it purely passive?

Of course, the first or principal cause has total priority over the second or instrumental cause. The second cause cannot be a cause except by the action of the first cause: "since the meaning is not that the second cause has no power except by the first: but that the second [cause] produces no effect itself, except by the concurrence of the first."[18]

In the same way, the principal cause has total priority over the instrumental cause: a paintbrush cannot paint without the painter. But this does not mean that the instrumental cause is thereby stripped of all significance. It has its own proper action; Cajetan opposes Duns Scotus when the latter maintains that the instrumental cause must have no proper effect.[19] It is interesting that Cajetan noted this detail, since Luther would manifest the same tendency. He

---

[16] *SCG,* book III, chapter 70.

[17] Cf. Charles Journet, *Entretiens sur la grâce* (Saint-Maurice: Éditions S.-Augustin, 1969), 43–45.

[18] "Quoniam non est sensus quod causa secunda nullam virtutem habeat nisi primae: sed quod ipsa secunda nullum effectum producit, nisi virtute primae concurrente" (*In Summ. Theol.,* Ia, q. 19, a. 8, no. XIV).

[19] Cf. *In Summ. Theol.,* Ia, q. 45, a. 5, no. XIII: "Vult ergo primo, quod causa instrumentalis non oportet quod habeat actionem pro

then replies to Scotus's objection, stating that "the instrumental cause has its own proper action, which nevertheless
coincides materially with the action which it has as instrument of the agent."[20] Cajetan illustrates the effect of the
instrumental cause with the example of a scribe who cannot manage to make his letters the same, depending on
whether he uses a good or bad stylus: certainly the stylus
depends entirely on the one who is writing, but in a certain
way the one who is writing depends on his stylus.[21] The
difference between the stylus in relation to the scribe and
us in relation to God is that we are active instrumental
causes endowed with initiative (this difference being the
foundation of our moral responsibility).

The instrumental cause therefore possesses its own
proper action, without necessitating any opposition in relation to the principal cause, for it is precisely in its dependence on the principle cause that the instrumental cause
achieves its proper effect.

When these principles are applied to God and the creature,
the multiplicity of creaturely modes of action involves neither
an absence of divine action (which would be the case if second causes were left to themselves, independent from God[22]),
nor a transmutation of God within the rhythm of the

---

priam." Cajetan adds that Scotus then slightly nuances his position
on this statement.

[20] "[D]ico tamen quod causa instrumentalis habet actionem propriam,
coincidentem tamen materialiter cum actione quam habet ut instru-
mentum agentis" (*In Summ. Theol.*, Ia, q. 45, a. 5, no. XVI). On the
same topic See *In Summ. Theol.*, Ia, q. 105, a. 5, the whole commentary).

[21] *In Summ. Theol.*, Ia, q. 19, a. 8, no. VII (the example is rather
broadly developed in this whole number of the commentary).

[22] In which case they would no longer really be second causes, as for
example in the defect of grace due to sin, cf. Ia IIae, q. 112, a. 3, ad
2: "The first cause of the defect of grace is on our part; but the first
cause of the bestowal of grace is on God's."

world (which could be the case if everything were produced directly by God, with second causes having only an appearance of reality).

Another question arises: does the priority of the first or principal cause imply that it acts first, leaving the other cause to intervene later?

The terminology should not give the impression of temporal succession. The first cause is called first not because it is prior in time and thus separated from the second cause, but because it is first in a priority of nature, which is not chronological, since the two causes operate at the same time, the one in the other:

> [T]his priority, universally, is not according to a certain natural duration, as though the effect is reached in a natural instant by the first cause, and in another by the second, as the argument would propose.[23] But this occurs according to the independence and immediacy of power: since the first, by the immediacy of its power, attains the effect in a more independent and immediate manner than the second. Nevertheless, it is in the same instant of time that the effect is attained by each of the two.[24]

---

[23] I.e. Scotus's argument, to which he is responding.

[24] "illa prioritas, universaliter, non est secundum aliquam quasi durationem naturae, ut in uno instanti naturae effectus attingatur a prima causa, et in alio a secunda, ut arguens imaginatur. Sed est secundum independentiam et immediationem virtutis: quia prior independentius et immediatius, immediatione virtutis, attingit effectum, quam secunda. In eodem tamen instanti naturae, effectus ab utraque attingitur" (*In Summ. Theol.*, Ia, q. 14, a. 13, no. XXIII). Cf. also *In Summ. Theol.*, Ia, q. 19, a. 8, no. XV: "Illa enim propositio assumpta non est sic intelligenda, quasi sit aliqua duratio naturae, in cuius primo instanti causa prima respiciat effectum, et in secundo causa secunda: puerilis enim hic est sensus; ex quo tamen consequentia processisse videtur. Sed est intelligenda quoad independentiam et intimitatem: attingit enim prima causa effectum

Today, this metaphysical perspective is not the first that might leap to mind. Nevertheless, it corresponds to simple experience: when I write a text, the pen is writing the whole text at the same time as I am, not an instant afterward; but I remain prior in this action, because the pen would not be able to write on its own.

Let us summarize the significance of the Thomistic understanding of causes. An act accomplished by man is also accomplished by God. God and man accomplish it simultaneously, each one 100 percent, because the two authors of the action are situated at two different levels of being, somewhat as when a man uses an instrument. Man can act, and what is more, act with his freedom, because God gives it to him. In such a perspective, it makes no sense to see human action as though in concurrence with God's action.

The Relation of Causes in the Sacrament of Penance According to Cajetan and Luther

The debate between Thomists and Scotists which we have just summarized clarifies Cajetan's reaction to the theology of the sacrament of Penance which he found in Luther's writings at the time of their encounter in 1518.

Among the problems which Cajetan identifies in those works of Luther which were accessible to him, I think the most crucial one concerns the sacrament of Penance: not its existence, which Luther did not call into question at that moment (as he would later on,[25] although the sacrament's

---

secundae et independentius et intimius quam secunda . . . et propterea dicitur respicere prius."

[25] For example, because his affinity to baptism prevents him from seeing it as a sacrament in itself (cf. Otto Hermann Pesch, *Die Theologie der Rechtfertigung*, 350), and because of his opposition to contrition (cf. Laurentius Klein, *Evangelisch-lutherische Beichte: Lehre und Praxis*, vol. 5 of *Konfessionskundliche und kontroverstheologische Studien* [Paderborn: Bonifacius-Druckerei, 1961], 22).

existence would be retained under article 11 of the *Augsburg Confession*, open to varying interpretation), but its significance. Behind this issue stands the wider issue of the effect of the sacraments in the New Covenant. Luther's opposition to the doctrine that the sacraments of the New Covenant confer grace would be the first point which Leo X condemned on June 15, 1520, in the Bull *Exsurge Domine*.[26] This issue cannot be understood without reference to the disputes over Penance.

Who forgives sins, Luther asks, God or the priest? He replies that "even if the remission of guilt takes place through the infusion of grace before the remission of the priest, this infusion is of such a nature and is so hidden under the form of wrath that man is more uncertain about grace when it is present than when it was absent; for the Scripture says, 'accordingly his footprints are not recognized' [Ps 77:19], and 'by paths his feet have not trod' [Isa 41:3]. So as a general rule we are not sure of the remission of guilt, except through the judgment of the priest."[27] In other words, God alone forgives sins, but in order for the penitent to be at peace, he must receive a declaration from the priest stating that forgiveness has been granted to him. Thus God alone, and not the priest, forgives sins.

This sacramental theology calls for two comments. First of all, it is deeply rooted in the reformer's personal history,

---

[26] Denz. 1451.

[27] "licet remissio culpae fiat per infusionem gratiae ante remissionem sacerdotis, talis tamen est infusio gratiae et ita sub forma irae abscondita (siquidem vestigia eius non cognoscuntur ps. lxxvi. Et semita in pedibus eius non apparet. Isa: xli), ut homo incertior sit de gratia, cum fuerit ipsa praesens, quam cum est absens. Ideo ordine generali non est nobis certa remissio culpae nisi per iudicium sacerdotis" (*Resolutiones disputationum de indulgentiarum virtute*, Concl. VII, WA 1, p. 541; translation: LW 31, 101). Cf. also *Resolutiones*, Concl. VII, pp. 539–45, Concl. VI, pp. 538–39, Concl. LXXVI, pp. 622–23, Concl. XXXVIII, p. 593.

including his liberation from scruples in Confession.[28] Second, Luther could believe that he was following a traditional point of view, that is, Peter Lombard's. Since Lombard, however, theology had benefited from certain clarifications, which the Council of Florence had adopted, stating that the sacrament is an absolution by the ministry of the priest, not a declaration of a prior absolution by God: "The form of this sacrament is the words of absolution spoken by the priest who has authority to absolve (. . .). The effect of this sacrament is absolution from sins."[29]

In his theology of the sacrament of Penance, Luther relies on Biel (and similar authors), this time not as the opponent against whom he is in reaction, but as the author

---

[28] Cf. Marc Lienhard, *Martin Luther: Un temps, une vie, un message*, 3rd ed., Histoire et Société 21r (Geneva: Labor et Fides, 1991), 38–39 [here translated from French]: "Luther's preceptor in the monastery seemed to have greatly helped Luther for a while by ordering him to believe in absolution. Reading St. Bernard was also of some help: there Luther found the idea that man is incapable of acquiring salvation, as well as the invitation to entrust himself to the suffering Christ. Above all, the role played by Staupitz, the vicar general of the Augustinian order, should be mentioned. According to various later testimonies from Luther, the former was principally responsible for soothing Luther's anguish concerning predestination. 'Staupitz said to me: "Those who wish to discuss predestination would be better off to leave it alone; they should begin by thinking of the wounds of Christ and should place Christ before their eyes. Then predestination would no longer be an issue, because God destined his son to suffer for sinners" (WA Tr 2, p. 227, no. 1820).' Did Staupitz simply want to draw attention to the redemptive death of Christ, which manifested the grace of God and dispelled fear? Was he also trying to say that for believers, following the suffering Christ, doubts are a sign chosen by God? The question cannot be resolved. In any case, Luther committed himself to this latter point of view. He integrated fear into his theology of the cross; fear would become the other face of faith, in the same way that God the Judge would be perceived in relation to the God of love."

[29] Council of Florence, *Decree for the Armenians* (November 22nd, 1439), Denz. 1323; *The Christian Faith*, 1612, Cf. Ia, q. 84, a. 3.

of the theology which he has accepted. In rejecting the Thomistic solution, according to which grace can be given in anticipation of the true desire for absolution, Biel disconnects the pardon bestowed by the Church from the pardon bestowed by God:

> The power of the keys extends to remission and retention of the fault, not in the eyes of God, but in the eyes of the Church. The first part is evident from the preceding conclusion, since the sin is not remitted, but it is presupposed already remitted by God. The second part is evident from what the Master . . . says: 'Since, although someone may be absolved in the eyes of God, he is nevertheless not considered absolved in the eyes of the Church except through the judgment of the priest.'[30]

This can be recognized as what would later become Luther's position. This disjunction between the action of God and the action of the priest intervenes not only in the sacrament of Penance, but also in Biel's general theory of the sacraments: "it should not be said that there is in the sacraments of the new law some supernatural virtue through which they would possess the status of cause, in relation to the sacramental effect."[31] In this, Biel explicitly

---

[30] "Tertia conclusio: Potestas clavium extendit se ad remissionem et retentionem culpae non coram Deo, sed in facie ecclesiae. Prima pars patet ex praecedenti conclusione, quia non remittit peccatum, sed remissum a Deo praesupponit. Secunda pars patet per *Magistrum* distinctione praesenti cap. 6 dicentem: 'Quia etsi aliquis apud Deum sit solutus, non tamen in facie ecclesiae solutus habetur nisi per iudicium sacerdotis'" (CCQLS, L. IV/2, dist. 18, quaestio 1, art. 2, concl. 3, vol. IV/2, p. 524). The last quote is taken from the Commentary on the Sentences of Peter Lombard (IV, d. 18, c. 6, n. 186).

[31] "Conclusion quarta: In sacramentis novae legis non est ponenda virtus supernaturalis, per quam respectu sacramentalis effectus eis conveniat ratio causalis" (CCQLS, L. IV/1, dist. 1, quaestio 1, art. 2, conclusio 4, vol. IV/1, p. 23). The term "sacraments of the new law"

opposes St. Thomas, according to whom "[w]e must needs say that in some way the sacraments of the New Law cause grace."[32] The principal argument which Biel provides in support of his thesis is that "no perfection of the spirit informs the body. Otherwise, intellection and volition, science, grace, and charity can inform a stone as a subject."[33] The reformers would later experience a similar difficulty in placing spirit and matter on common ground.[34]

In examining Luther's theology, the first thing which came to Cajetan's mind was the distinction between principal cause and instrumental cause. In his *Sermo de penitentia*,[35] delivered before Easter 1518,[36] Luther asserts, "It is sufficient for the sacraments of the New Law to be efficacious signs of grace, if you believe, and nothing more."[37] Did Cajetan recognize this statement[38] as one of the objections cited by Thomas in the *Summa*: "It seems that the sacraments are not

---

designates the sacraments of the Christian economy, as distinguished from the signs of the Mosaic law.

[32] IIIa, q. 62, a. 1. For Biel, cf. CCQLS, L. IV/1, dist. 1, quaestio 1, art. 2, conclusio 4, vol. IV/1, p. 23: "Haec conclusio ponitur contra tertium dictum sancti Thomae, quo ponit virtutem quandam spiritualem supernaturalem in sacramentis, per quam concurrunt active instrumentaliter ad dispositionem et dispositive ad gratiam."

[33] "Quia nulla perfectio spiritus informat corpus. Alioquin intellectio et volitio, scientia, gratia, caritas possunt subiective informare lapidem" (CCQLS, L. IV/1, dist. 1, quaestio 1, art. 2, conclusio 4, vol. IV/1, p. 23). Here, the term "inform" should be understood in the sense of "giving form" to something, according to Aristotelian hylomorphism.

[34] And perhaps Calvin also had difficulty understanding how the sacraments of the New Covenant differ from the signs of the Old Covenant; cf. Bernard Sesboüé, *Pour une théologie oecuménique* (Paris: Cerf, 1990), 178.

[35] WA 1, pp. 317–24.

[36] WA 1, pp. 239–46.

[37] "Satis sit quod sacramenta novae legis sunt efficatia signa gratiae, si credis, et non amplius" (*Sermo de penitentia*, WA 1, p. 324).

[38] Except for the theology of faith which Luther adds.

the cause of grace. For it seems that the same thing is not both sign and cause: since the nature of sign appears to be more in keeping with an effect. But a sacrament is a sign of grace. Therefore it is not its cause"?[39] Thomas's reply made use of the distinction between levels of causality:

> The principal cause cannot properly be called a sign of its effect, even though the latter be hidden and the cause itself sensible and manifest. But an instrumental cause, if manifest, can be called a sign of a hidden effect, for this reason, that it is not merely a cause but also in a measure an effect in so far as it is moved by the principal agent. And in this sense the sacraments of the New Law are both cause and signs. Hence, too, is it that, to use the common expression, "they effect what they signify." From this it is clear that they perfectly fulfil the conditions of a sacrament; being ordained to something sacred, not only as a sign, but also as a cause.[40]

Cajetan's response to Luther adheres exactly to St. Thomas: "it is one and the same remission of sin which the priest accomplished ministerially and which God accomplishes by his own authority; in the same way, God accomplishes by his own authority the same conversion of bread into the Body of Christ that the words of Christ effect through the lips of the priest."[41] To state in this way that

---

[39] IIIa, q. 62, a. 1, objection 1.

[40] IIIa, q. 62, a. 1, ad 1. It is interesting to note that in his theology of instrumental causality, in addition to his theology of dispositive causality, St. Thomas is reacting not only against sacramental theologians, but also against a philosopher like Avicenna (it would be interesting to compare this Muslim philosopher's vision of Providence with Luther's), assisted by Aristotle and Averrhoes; cf. H.-D. Dondain, "A propos d'Avicenne et de saint Thomas," *RT* 51 (1951): 441–53.

[41] I will be quoting Cajetan according to the following edition: Charles Morerod, *Cajetan et Luther en 1518,* opuscule XI.6, vol. 1, p. 347.

one and the same action can be accomplished by God and by the priest, each at his own level, implies a whole metaphysics of the relation of causes, without which the debate between these two theologians can never be understood. Moreover, when Cajetan later addressed question 62 of the Tertia Pars, quoted above, in his Commentary on the Tertia Pars of the Summa (completed in 1522), he too analyzed the question in Thomas's terms, according to the relationship between principal cause and instrumental cause.[42] His discussion touched on this point because at the time, he was responding to Scotus. In referring to Luther, he did not need to be as precise, but he could not help noting the similarity in the questions.

The Foundations of the Essence of the Church

Luther, and all of Protestantism in his wake, tends to relativize the importance of ecclesiastical structures, denying their divine institution as understood by the Catholic Church.[43] This relativization of the Church can be understood only in connection with his theology of justification. We should also note that the way in which Luther expresses his theology of justification depends on his implicit metaphysical framework, or, more precisely, on his understanding

---

[42] Cf. *In Summ. Theol.*, IIIa, q. 62, a. 1, the whole commentary.

[43] See for example one of the most recent works on the question: Anthony Levi, *Renaissance and Reformation*, 285: "Luther's attack on the power structures of the papacy and the bitterness of anti-curial feeling in Germany led inevitably to a series of attempts, which remained uncoordinated, to clear away the totality of the church's hierarchically constituted juridical, administrative, and financial systems. The implications of the abolition of ecclesiastical structures for the social organization of religious activity required thinking through. The essential question concerned whether or how far the church's hierarchical structure and the associated sacramental system were of divine institution."

of the relation between divine and human causalities. This is
what Cajetan wished to point out, from the standpoint of
sacramental theology.

For Cajetan, it is essential for all sacramental theology to
understand the relation between God and his creatures in
terms of subordination and not concurrence. He is careful
to show that Luther's positions on Penance could be similarly applied to Baptism and the Eucharist,[44] a possibility
which he later mentioned explicitly when discussing the
Zwinglians in 1525:

> It does not follow from the fact that our sins are destroyed
> only by the death of Christ, that the application of Christ's
> death to us does not destroy sins. For just as the fact that
> the artisan makes a sphere does not exclude the artisan's
> instruments with which he makes the sphere; so, the fact
> that only the death of Christ destroys our sins does not
> exclude the sacraments of the Church, which are the
> instruments through which the death of Christ is applied
> to us; otherwise one ought to suppress from the Creed, "I
> confess one baptism for the forgiveness of sins." Indeed, if
> the fact that the death of Christ alone destroys our sins
> necessitated the exclusion of the sacraments, baptism too
> would be excluded from the destruction of sins.[45]

---

44 Cf. the Augsburg opuscula, in my edition (Cajetan et Luther en
   1518), §§XI.7 and XI.10. A. Landgraf, "Grundlagen für ein Verständnis der Busslehre der Früh- und Hochscholastik," Zeitschrift
   für Theologie und Kirche [hereafter ZKT] (1927): 187–88, is sur-
   prised to note that the arguments used historically to question the
   validity of the sacrament of Penance have never been used for Baptism, although they could be applied to Baptism in the same way.

45 "Ex hoc enim, quod sola mors Christi nostra delet peccata, non
   sequitur, Ergo applicatio mortis Christi ad nos non delet peccata.
   Sicut namque ex hoc, quod solus artifex facit spheram, non
   excluduntur instrumenta artificis, quibus spheram operatur: ita ex
   hoc quod sola mors Christi delet nostra peccata non excluduntur
   sacramenta Ecclesiae, quae sunt instrumenta, quibus mors Christi

Effectively, if the salvation won by Christ alone cannot be transmitted by any other instrument than himself, the whole life of the Church—and even the Bible—should be abolished.

---

applicatur ad nos, alioquin delere oportet ex symbolo, Confiteor unum baptisma in remissionem peccatorum. Si enim ex hoc, quod sola mors Christi delet nostra peccata, excluderentur sacramenta, Baptismus quoque excluditur a deletione peccatorum" (Thomas de Vio Cardinalis Caietanus, *Instructio nuntii circa errores libelli de Cena Domini* sive *De erroribus contingentibus in Eucharistiae sacramento*, no. 42, Franciscus A. von Gunten, OP editionem curavit [Rome: Apud Pontificium Athenaeum "Angelicum," 1962], 57).

CHAPTER 3

Divine and Human Causality in Luther and Calvin

IN 1518, Cajetan and Luther were engaged in a debate over sacramental causality. Was this a marginal and insignificant argument, foreign to the subsequent evolution of Luther's theology? Or was it specific to Luther but absent from other trends within the Reformation or its later history?

First, we will verify whether the theme of causality is still present in Luther's theology after 1518, referring primarily to his programmatic work, the treatise on the bondage of the will, and then to his theology of the two kingdoms.

Second, we will examine the same theme in Calvin, beginning with his understanding of justification. It is on this point, as a direct result of their understanding of causality, that the two reformers and their respective traditions are closest to each other:

> [T]he reformed disciples of John Calvin in the 17th century were conscious of differing with the Lutherans on numerous scores; but they recognized that they were all united in this doctrine of justification by faith, which was the foundation of the whole Reformation: indeed, the central doctrine

of Christianity and the principal point on which Protestantism and Roman Catholicism differ.[1]

Even when contemporary Protestants began to distance themselves from the reformers, reference to the doctrine of justification remained as a stamp of their origin and identity. This point is clear enough, in terms of theology. We will examine it here as a philosophically constituted principle of thought.

The *Bondage of the Will* According to Luther

Luther began to promulgate his main theses in his commentary on the famous Ninety-Five Theses of 1517, that is, the *Resolutiones disputationum de indulgentiarum virtute*, which he sent to the pope on May 30, 1518.[2] Sensitive to a pastoral situation which was not particularly admirable, Luther could not acquiesce to the view of indulgences as an assurance of eternal salvation. "Those who believe that they can be certain of their salvation because they have indulgence letters will be eternally damned, together with their teachers."[3] He develops the same idea regarding the efficacy of the sacraments, particularly the sacrament of Penance. Far from being the necessary condition for the forgiveness of one's sins, contrition can even lead to damnation those who place their trust in it rather than in God: "True contrition is

---

[1] Jaroslav Pelikan, *La Tradition chrétienne: Histoire du développement de la doctrine*, vol. 4: *La réforme de l'Eglise et du dogme*, Théologiques (Paris: PUF, 1984), 136.

[2] *Resolutiones disputationum de indulgentiarum virtute*, with introduction, WA 1, pp. 522–628. Hereafter *Resolutiones*.

[3] *Resolutiones*, Concl. XXXII, WA 1, p. 587; translation from LW 31, 179.

not from us, but from the grace of God: consequently we must despair of ourselves and take refuge in his mercy."[4]

God does all, man does nothing. This concept is the goal of Luther's argument on contrition: he is not opposed to contrition, as long as it is effected through the grace of God, but he denies any human share in it.[5]

These theses, proclaimed at the symbolic start of the Reformation, would be developed in *De servo arbitrio* in 1525, in which Luther responds to *De libero arbitrio diatribe sive collatio*, published by Erasmus at Basel the previous year.[6] The issue at stake is whether it is possible for man to execute a choice vis-à-vis God in relation to his eternal salvation. Since Luther maintains that salvation is solely the work of grace and in no way a human work, he has to conclude that man cannot execute any choice which would give him an active part in this work of salvation. This is why he rejects the operation of free will within man's relation to God. Original sin destroyed free will, which, since that time, has been a word empty of meaning.

De servo arbitrio expresses Luther's understanding of the relationship between man and God. He considers it obvious that whatever man does, God does not do.

For Luther, this is not a minor question. It is at the heart of his vision of the Christian faith: "it is not irreverent, inquisitive, or superfluous, but essentially salutary and necessary for

---

4 "Contritio vera non est ex nobis, sed ex gratia dei: ideo desperandum de nobis et ad misericordiam eius confugiendum" (*Sermo de penitentia*, WA 1, p. 322).

5 It should be clarified that for Luther, contrition—as presented by his opponents—is not only harmful, but impossible: it is presumptuous to claim to know all one's sins (cf. his *Sermo de penitentia*, given before Easter 1518, WA 1, pp. 322–23).

6 For a presentation of these two works and their historical context, see Georges Chantraine, *Erasme et Luther: Libre et serf arbitre* (Paris: Editions Lethellieux; Namur: Presses Universitaires de Namur, 1981).

a Christian, to find out whether the will does anything or nothing in matters pertaining to eternal salvation. Indeed, as you should know, this is the cardinal issue between us, the point on which everything in this controversy turns. For what we are doing is to inquire what free choice can do, what it has done to it, and what is its relation to the grace of God. If we do not know these things, we shall know nothing at all of things Christian, and shall be worse than any heathen."[7] In these circumstances, those who uphold a different view are not only theologians of another school: "I wish the defenders of free choice would take warning at this point, and realize that when they assert free choice they are denying Christ."[8] Although Luther is utterly opposed to Erasmus, he commends him for having at least chosen a worthwhile topic for dispute: "I praise and commend you highly for this also, that unlike all the rest you alone have attacked the real issue, the essence of the matter in dispute, and have not wearied me with irrelevancies about the papacy, purgatory, indulgences, and such like trifles (for trifles they are rather than basic issues), with which almost everyone hitherto has gone hunting for me without success. You and you alone have seen the question on which everything hinges, and have aimed at the vital spot; for which I sincerely thank you."[9]

Luther believes he must deny free will because he implicitly holds as self-evident the principle that whatever man does, God does not do. Thus God is the cause of our salvation in its entirety, and to attribute to him only a part, even the quasi-totality, of salvation, would be to outrage his transcendence. If this is the case, then everything which is attributed to man in terms of salvation is stolen from God:

---

[7] *The Bondage of the Will,* LW 33, 35.
[8] Ibid., LW 33, 279.
[9] Ibid., LW 33, 294.

"you yourself [Erasmus] are aware that all the good in us is to be ascribed to God, and you assert this in your description of Christianity. But in asserting this, you are surely asserting also that the mercy of God alone does everything, and that your will does nothing, but rather is passive; otherwise, all is not ascribed to God."[10]

Then what part remains to human choice, at least in terms of salvation? None whatsoever: "As for the second paradox, that whatever is done by us is done not by free choice but of sheer necessity, let us look briefly at this and not permit it to be labeled most pernicious. What I say here is this: When it has been proved that salvation is beyond our own powers and devices, and depends on the work of God alone (as I hope to prove conclusively below in the main body of this disputation), does it not follow that when God is not present and at work in us everything we do is evil and we necessarily do what is of no avail for salvation?"[11] Without divine grace, man can only do the evil toward which he is now instinctively inclined, as a consequence of original sin:

> [W]hen a man is without the Spirit of God he does not do
> evil against his will, as if he were taken by the scruff of the
> neck and forced to it, like a thief or robber carried off
> against his will to punishment, but he does it of his own
> accord and with a ready will. And this readiness or will to
> act he cannot by his own powers omit, restrain, or change,
> but he keeps on willing and being ready; and even if he is
> compelled by external force to do something different, yet
> the will within him remains averse and he is resentful at
> whatever compels or resists it.[12]

---

10 Ibid., LW 33, 35.
11 Ibid., LW 33, 64.
12 Ibid., LW 33, 64.

If the Christian has any freedom, it is not as an act of free will, but as a consequence of grace working without free will:

> By contrast, if God works in us, the will is changed, and being gently breathed upon by the Spirit of God, it again wills and acts from pure willingness and inclination and of its own accord, not from compulsion, so that it cannot be turned another way by any opposition, nor be overcome or compelled even by the gates of hell, but it goes on willing and delighting in and loving the good, just as before it willed and delighted in and loved evil. This again is proved by experience, which shows how invincible and steadfast holy men are, who when force is used to compel them to other things are thereby all the more spurred on to will the good, just as fire is fanned into flames rather than extinguished by the wind. So not even here is there any free choice, or freedom to turn oneself in another direction or will something different, so long as the Spirit and grace of God remain in a man.[13]

If man cannot choose to establish himself for or against God, why then do men have different religious attitudes? This is a divine secret, and we should not seek to unlock it: "why does he not at the same time change the evil wills that he moves? This belongs to the secrets of his majesty, where his judgments are incomprehensible."[14] God is as free and

---

[13] Ibid., LW 33, 65.

[14] Ibid., LW 33, 180. Cf. also LW 33, 138–39: "why some are touched by the law and others are not, so that the former accept and the latter despise the offered grace, is another question and one not dealt with by Ezekiel in this passage. For he is here speaking of the preached and offered mercy of God, not of that hidden and awful will of God whereby he ordains by his own counsel which and what sort of persons he wills to be recipients and partakers of his preached and offered mercy. This will is not to be inquired into, but reverently adored as by far the most awe-inspiring secret of the Divine Majesty, reserved for himself alone and forbidden to us much more religiously than any number of Corycian caverns."

sovereign in the work of our salvation as in our creation: we do not participate in either event, and everything can be reduced to the design of a God who knows apart from us what we are going to do.[15]

Thus man's destiny is determined apart from him, depending on whether God sets a man apart for himself or hands him over to another master, Satan: "the human will is placed between the two like a beast of burden. If God rides it, it wills and goes where God wills. (. . .) If Satan rides it, it wills and goes where Satan wills; nor can it choose to run to either of the two riders or to seek him out, but the riders themselves contend for the possession and control of it."[16]

If this is true, why does God give commandments to man? Consistent with his exegesis of Romans 8, Luther replies simply that "[t]he whole meaning and purpose of the law is simply to furnish knowledge, and that of nothing but sin; it is not to reveal or confer any power. For this knowledge is not power, nor does it confer power, but it instructs and shows that there is no power there, and how great a weakness there is,"[17] at least in what is done without grace. Georges Chantraine points out that if man is thus deprived of the capacity to respond, the Lutheran conception of the Word seems more like a monologue than a dialogue.[18]

Today's mentality values freedom very highly. Reacting against this mentality, which was already being promulgated by Erasmus, Luther noted its limitations: the freedom of the Christian, founded in God, is in reality far

---

[15] Cf. ibid., LW 33, 191: "just as we do not come into being by our own will, but by necessity, so we do not do anything by right of free choice, but as God has foreknown and as he leads us to act by his infallible and immutable counsel and power."

[16] Ibid., LW 33, 65–66.

[17] Ibid., LW 33, 127.

[18] Cf. Chantraine, *Erasme et Luther*, 419.

superior to a kind of moral indifference which is sometimes confused with freedom. And although Luther's approach may easily be mocked, it was a courageous and painful affirmation of divine transcendence.

But is there no other means of proclaiming divine transcendence than the one which Luther chose? Is it necessary to exclude human action in order to safeguard divine action? For St. Thomas, the fact that a creature accomplishes an act is no obstacle to God's accomplishing 100 percent of this same act. But Luther completely misunderstands this type of relation between causes. His ironic suggestions upon meeting Erasmus show that for him, the action of created causality presupposes the inaction of divine causality: "At another the First Cause does everything, and at yet another it acts through secondary causes while remaining itself at rest."[19]

We must add that Luther was motivated solely by a desire to defend the transcendence of God. His painful personal experience of searching for an assurance of salvation is deeply implicated in this question. Like many Christians at the end of the Middle Ages, Luther was tormented by the prospect of salvation or damnation, and at first had tried, without success, to find peace through religious practices. He finally found this peace (or at least he had more success searching for it) in faith in the salvific action of God. Thus, where human works were clearly powerless, he drew consolation from God's promise: "this is the one supreme consolation of Christians in all adversities, to know that God does not lie, but does all things immutably, and that his will can neither be resisted nor changed nor hindered."[20] Personal experience and theological reasoning are closely connected.

---

[19] *The Bondage of the Will,* LW 33, 185.
[20] Ibid., LW 33, 43.

Luther's understanding of causality is expressed in another theme of his work: the relationship between the two kingdoms.

The Separation of Two Kingdoms in Luther

If Luther fiercely denies free will in the realm of salvation, he does not deny it in other areas. Although he deems it preferable not to use the term, he recognizes that free will can be acknowledged in everything which does not concern salvation:

> [I]f we are unwilling to let this term go altogether—though that would be the safest and most God-fearing thing to do—let us at least teach men to use it honestly, so that free choice is allowed to man only with respect to what is beneath him and not what is above him. That is to say, a man should know that with regard to his faculties and possessions he has the right to use, to do, or to leave undone, according to his own free choice, though even this is controlled by the free choice of God alone, who acts in whatever way he pleases. On the other hand in relation to God, or in matters pertaining to salvation or damnation, a man has no free choice, but is a captive, subject and slave either of the will of God or the will of Satan.[21]

Thus the Christian is divided between two kingdoms,[22] the divine and the human:

> A prince may well be a Christian, but he must not govern as a Christian; and insofar as he reigns he is not called a Christian, but a prince. . . . For insofar as he is a Christian, the Gospel teaches him that he should not do evil to anyone,

---

[21] *The Bondage of the Will*, LW 33, 70.
[22] For a brief presentation of this theme, see Lienhard, *Martin Luther*, 246–58.

neither punishing nor in speech, but that he must pardon
everyone, and suffer whatever hardship or injustice happens
to him. This (I say), is the lesson for a Christian. But this
would not make good government, if you wished to preach
it also to the prince. On the contrary, he must say: I leave
my state as Christian between God and myself. . . . But
above, or besides, this state, I have another state or function
in the world: that of being a prince.[23]

Fr. Congar believes that this theology of two kingdoms can
even be found in Luther's Christology[24]—not surprisingly,
since the existence of difficulties in understanding the relationship between God and man implies that there are difficulties first of all in understanding Christ in the life of
the Church.

The previous paragraph may be something of a caricature
of Luther's thought on this topic, but it must be acknowledged that on a long-term basis, his writings would promote

---

23 "Ein Fürst kan wol ein Christen sein, aber als ein Christ mus er
nicht regieren: und nach dem er regiret, heisst er nicht ein Christ
sondern ein Fürst . . . Denn nach dem er ein Christ ist, leret in das
Euangelium das er niemand sol leid thun, nicht straffen noch
rechen, sondern idermann vergeben, und was im leid odder unrecht
geschicht sol er leiden. Das ist (sage ich) eines Christen lectio, Aber
das würde nicht ein gut regiment machen, wenn du dem Fürsten
woltest also predigen, Sondern so mus er sagen: Meinem Christen-
stand lasse ich gehen zwischen Gott und mir. . . . Aber über odder
neben dem habe ich inn der welt einen andern stand odder ampt:
das ich ein Fürst bin" (Luther, Wochenpredigten über Matt. 5–7,
1530/2, Druck 1532, WA 32, 440).

24 Cf. Yves Congar, *Martin Luther: Sa foi, sa Réforme,* Cogitatio Fidei
119 (Paris: Cerf, 1983), 130 [here translated from French]: "This is
the whole idea of the two Reiche. In the area of salvation, in whatever
has any worth coram Deo, God alone operates efficaciously in Christ,
who is inseparably God." Gabriella Cotta comes to the same conclusion (*La nascita dell'individualismo politico,* 40). On this topic, cf.
André Birmelé, *Le Salut en Jésus-Christ dans les dialogues oecuméniques,*
298–302; Sesboüé, *Pour une théologie oecuménique,* 62, 179–80.

in his disciples a detachment between temporal life and religious faith, no matter how fervent this faith might have originally been.[25] Furthermore, civic life is not the only thing which is separated from the religious dimension: man too, bound to depart from himself in a religious journey focused on his own negativity, paradoxically finds himself at the center. Gabriella Cotta admirably summarizes the fact that Luther's thought "ends by producing a result opposite to the one which the Reformer was desperately seeking; and in the void left by a henceforth inaccessible divinity, it exalts the centrality of man and thus of history."[26]

Before commenting on the impact of Luther's thought in subsequent centuries, however, we will present Calvin's theological understanding of the relationship between divine and human causalities.

---

[25] On this point, Calvin's goal was different, illustrated by his own seizure of temporal life in Geneva.

[26] "finisce per produrre un risultato che è l'opposto di quello esasperatamente cercato dal Riformatore e, nel vuoto di un divino ormai irraggiungibile, enfatizza la centralità dell'umano, e dunque della storia" (Cotta, *La nascita dell'individualismo politico*, 41). Cf. also ibid., 29–30: "Poiché l'assoluta incapacità naturale di riconoscere la positività del bene, è solo a partire dal proprio sé decaduto, che, paradossalmente, si può intraprendere l'itinerario della salvezza. Carenze ontologiche così insuperabili, proprio perché del tutto strutturali, non sono altro che il necessario correlato del nascondimento di Dio: 'Dio si rivela solamente nascondendosi' e, di conseguenza, 'anche rivelato, resta sempre nascosto.' A un Dio totalmente nascosto e inconoscibile—la cui natura è però quella di bene infinito—non può non corrispondere altro che un uomo totalmente privato della possibilità di una Sua conoscenza, perché totalmente peccatore." Cf. finally ibid, 45: "spogliati d'ogni somiglianza/analogia con il Creatore, e da ogni conseguente possibilità di partecipazione alla dimensione dell' essere, fino a questo momento generalmente data per scontata, sia pure nelle diverse teorizzazioni, gli uomini acquistano un'autonomia, per quanto riguarda la vita della carne, puramente umana, mai pensata fino allora."

Calvin

Although Calvin did not agree with Luther in all respects, he shared the most fundamental presupposition of Luther's thought, in terms of the subject of this study. We will highlight the similarity with a few texts from his major work, *Institutes of the Christian Religion.*[27]

Before plunging to the heart of the matter, we will deal with some preliminary themes which might obscure our main question. The first is Calvin's attitude toward philosophy. The second is the concept of the Church in Calvin's thought.

Before seeking the common points between the two reformers, it should be noted that Calvin's attitude toward philosophers (with a certain predilection for Plato) is more moderate than Luther's. For instance, he sees real merit in their study of the soul.[28] Praise flows from his pen which would be sought for in vain from Luther: "Whenever we come upon these matters in secular writers, let that admirable light of truth shining in them teach us that the mind of man, though fallen and perverted from its wholeness, is nevertheless clothed and ornamented with God's excellent gifts. If we regard the Spirit of God as the whole fountain of truth, we shall neither reject the truth itself, nor despise it wherever it shall appear, unless we dishonour the Spirit of God."[29] Calvin attributes these accomplishments

---

[27] John Calvin, *Institutes of the Christian Religion,* Library of Christian Classics, vols. XX–XXI (Philadelphia: Westminster Press; London: S.C.M. Press, 1967).

[28] Cf. ICR I.XV.6: "I leave it to the philosophers to discuss these faculties [of the soul] in their subtle way. (. . .) I, indeed, agree that the things they teach are true, not only enjoyable, but also profitable to learn, and skilfully assembled by them."

[29] Ibid., II.II.15.

to the general grace of God, which limits the effects of corruption,[30] and which accounts for the virtues of pagans.[31]

Nevertheless, Calvin should not be made out to be a beatific admirer of philosophers. For him, intelligence is corrupted,[32] and without grace, it can know neither the social order[33] nor the practical or liberal arts,[34] nor, least of all, God.[35] The philosophers believed that free will survived because they were ignorant of the Fall.[36] The Epicureans are a plague.[37] The Fathers (except perhaps Augustine) followed the philosophers too much, because they were intimidated by the mockeries of the latter, and because they were afraid that moral apathy would result from the idea that there is nothing for man to undertake.[38]

Catholics often view the Reformation in its Calvinist form as being particularly evasive in terms of ecclesiology. Hence, one might suppose that the question of the Church is the fundamental basis for the differences between Catholics and Reformed, whereas the ecclesial dimension is more obviously present among Lutherans.

Calvin's theology certainly does grant considerable importance to the Church, which he discusses in context of the preaching of God's instrument, the Word: "we must consider their special value [of the exhortations] for believers, in whom (as the Lord does all things through his Spirit) he does not neglect the instrument of his Word but makes effective

---

[30] Cf. ibid., II.17.
[31] Cf. ibid., II.III.3–4.
[32] Cf. ibid., II.II.12–25.
[33] Cf. ibid., II.II.13.
[34] Cf. ibid., II.II.14.
[35] Cf. ibid., II.II.18–20.
[36] Cf. ibid., I.XV.8.
[37] Cf. ibid. I.XVI.4.
[38] Cf. ibid. II.II.4.

use of it."[39] Consequently, preaching and the preachers of
the Word, as well as the sacraments, are also instruments,
through which God comes to us in consideration of what we
are.[40] This preaching is endowed with a kind of infallibility:
"so long as we continue in the bosom of the Church, we are
sure that the truth will remain with us."[41]

A Church does exist, then, and it plays a role in man's
relationship with God. Calvin's Catechism highlights its
importance:

SCHOLAR   Next comes the fourth part, in which we confess
that we believe in one Holy Catholic Church.

MASTER   What is the Church?

SCHOLAR   The body and society of believers whom God hath
predestined to eternal life.

MASTER   Is it necessary to believe this article also?

SCHOLAR   Yes, verily, if we would not make the death of Christ
without effect, and set at nought all that has hitherto been said. For the one effect resulting from all
is, that there is a Church.[42]

---

[39] Ibid., II.V.5.

[40] Cf. ibid., IV.I.1: "God, in accommodation to our infirmity, has
added such helps, and secured the effectual preaching of the gospel,
by depositing this treasure with the Church. He has appointed pas-
tors and teachers, by whose lips he might edify his people (Eph.
4:11); he has invested them with authority, and, in short, omitted
nothing that might conduce to holy consent in the faith, and to
right order. In particular, he has instituted sacraments, which we feel
by experience to be most useful helps in fostering and confirming
our faith."

[41] Ibid., IV.I.3. Of course, this infallibility is limited to what is necessary for salvation and what the Word of God teaches (cf. ibid.,
IV.VIII.13), and no new articles of faith must be introduced (cf.
ibid., IV.VIII.9), but nonetheless a sort of "magisterium" does exist,
a human instrument of teaching, enjoying divine guarantee.

[42] "Q. Qu'est-ce que l'Eglise catholique? R. C'est la compagnie des
fidèles, que Dieu a ordonnés et élus à la vie éternelle. Q. Est-il

But what is the Church's role in human actions?

To a certain extent, Calvin still recognizes the possible significance of instrumentality, as we saw above in the archetypal case of the Word of God, to which the Reformation always avoids applying the principles which it reserves for all the other means of salvation.

Calvin even upholds the existence of lower causes: "The Christian, then, being most fully persuaded, that all things come to pass by the dispensation of God, and that nothing happens fortuitously, will always direct his eye to him as the principal cause of events, at the same time paying due regard to inferior causes in their own place."[43] Sometimes his statements seem almost identical to St. Thomas's:

> At the same time, the Christian will not overlook inferior causes. For, while he regards those by whom he is benefited as ministers of the divine goodness, he will not, therefore, pass them by, as if their kindness deserved no gratitude, but feeling sincerely obliged to them, will willingly confess the obligation, and endeavour, according to his ability, to return it. In fine, in the blessings which he receives, he will revere and extol God as the principal author, but will also honour men as his ministers, and perceive, as is the truth, that by the will of God he is under obligation to those, by whose hand God has been pleased to show him kindness.[44]

Thus Calvin, much more than Luther, retains an appreciation for instrumentality. Nevertheless, he does not reach a clear or complete understanding of it, because he tends to

---

nécessaire de croire cet article? R.- Oui, si nous ne voulons rendre la mort de Jésus-Christ infructueuse et tout ce qui en a été dit, inutile: car le fruit qui en procède, c'est l'Eglise" (*Le Catéchisme de Jean Calvin*, [Paris: éd. Je Sers, 1934], 15th sect., p. 43). Translation, *The Geneva Catechism* (from: http://www.ondoctrine.com/2cal0504.htm).

43 ICR, I.XVII.6.

44 Ibid., I.XVII.9.

think that upholding human causality amounts to dividing
actions between God and man: "they so apportion things
between God and man that God by His power inspires in
man a movement by which he can act in accordance with
the nature implanted in him, but He regulates His own
actions by the plan of His will. Briefly, they mean that the
universe, men's affairs, and men themselves are governed by
God's might but not by His determination."[45] This concern leads him, like Luther, to devalue human action in
favor of God.

Thus, although he does retain the existence of ministry
in the Church, he is careful to point out the limits of the
minister and attribute everything to God:

> that he allows no more to ministers is obvious from other
> passages. "So then neither is he that planteth anything, nei-
> ther he that watereth; but God that giveth the increase" (1
> Cor. 3:7). Again, "I laboured more abundantly than they
> all: yet not I, but the grace of God which was with me"
> (1Cor. 15:10). And it is indeed necessary to keep these sen-
> tences in view, since God, in ascribing to himself the illu-
> mination of the mind and renewal of the heart, reminds us
> that it is sacrilege for man to claim any part of either to
> himself. Still every one who listens with docility to the
> ministers whom God appoints, will know by the beneficial
> result, that for good reason God is pleased with this
> method of teaching, and for good reason has laid believers
> under this modest yoke.[46]

If the ministers of the sacrament claim that God is appeased
by their oblation, they are usurping divine authority, and

---

45 Ibid., I.XVI.4. Cf. also III.XXIV.I.
46 Ibid., IV.I.6. On the humility of believers as the ultimate goal of
   human authority in the Church, cf. also IV.III.1.

their priesthood is sacrilegious.[47] It is not surprising that Calvin, discussing the intercession of the saints, further concludes that "it is manifest sacrilege to offer prayer to others[48] than God.

This relativization of the role of ministers is supported by a general principle which closely resembles Luther's: "It is, therefore, robbery from God to arrogate anything to ourselves, either in the will or the act";[49] "When we have entirely discarded all self-confidence, and trust solely in the certainty of his goodness, we are fit to apprehend and obtain the grace of God (. . .) for to whatever extent any man rests in himself, to the same extent he impedes the beneficence of God."[50] His theology of Divine Providence can view the normal course of nature only in terms of rivalry with God:

> [I]f God's governance is so extended to all his works, it is a childish cavil to enclose it within the stream of nature. Indeed, those as much defraud God of his glory as themselves of a most profitable doctrine who confine God's providence to such narrow limits as though he allowed all things by a free course to be borne along according to a universal law of nature.[51]

He applies this implicit principle to the sacraments as well:

> [T]he internal grace of the Spirit, as it is distinct from the external ministration, ought to be viewed and considered separately. God, therefore, truly performs whatever he promises and figures by signs; nor are the signs without

---

[47] Cf. ibid., IV.XIX, 28.
[48] Ibid., III.XX.27.
[49] Ibid., II.III.9.
[50] Ibid., III.XII.8.
[51] Ibid., I.XVI.3.

effect, for they prove that he is their true and faithful author. The only question here is, whether the Lord works by proper and intrinsic virtue (as it is called), or resigns his office to external symbols? We maintain, that whatever organs he employs detract nothing from his primary operation . . . we get rid of that fiction by which the cause of justification and the power of the Holy Spirit are included in elements as vessels and vehicles, and the special power which was overlooked is distinctly explained. Here, also, we ought to observe, that what the minister figures and attests by outward action, God performs inwardly, lest that which God claims for himself alone should be ascribed to mortal man.[52]

One may recognize the link between this general principle and the fear which Calvin expresses regarding the Eucharist: "The presence of Christ in the Supper we must hold to be such as neither affixes him to the element of bread, nor encloses him in bread, nor circumscribes him in any way (this would obviously detract from his celestial glory)."[53]

Calvin's position as presented above, like Luther's, is motivated by a desire to safeguard divine transcendence. This desire explicitly leads him to deny human participation: "so long as a man has any thing, however small, to say in his own defense, so long he deducts somewhat from the glory of God."[54] Calvin is clearly entrenched in a spiritual perspective:

When we have entirely discarded all self-confidence, and trust solely in the certainty of his goodness, we are fit to apprehend and obtain the grace of God. "When," (as Augustine says), "forgetting our own merits, we embrace the gifts of Christ, because if he should seek for merits in

---

[52] Ibid., IV.XIV.17.
[53] Ibid., IV.XVII.19.
[54] Ibid., III.XIII.1.

us we should not obtain his gifts," (August. de Verb. Apost. 8). With this Bernard admirably accords, comparing the proud who presume in the least on their merits, to unfaithful servants, who wickedly take the merit of a favor merely passing through them, just as if a wall were to boast of producing the ray which it receives through the window (Bernard, Serm. 13, in Cant). Not to dwell longer here, let us lay down this short but sure and general rule, That he is prepared to reap the fruits of the divine mercy who has thoroughly emptied himself, I say not of righteousness (he has none), but of a vain and blustering show of righteousness; for to whatever extent any man rests in himself, to the same extent he impedes the beneficence of God.[55]

Man is passive in the reception of the sacraments, as in his religious life in general, so that God can perform everything: "in receiving them [the sacraments] they do nothing which deserves praise, and that in this action (which in respect of them is merely passive) no work can be ascribed to them."[56]

A Christian, or indeed any religious man, cannot help but rejoice to hear someone singing the glory of God. All believers can identify with the intention which Calvin and Luther share. But must one necessarily accept their method for exalting divine transcendence—a method which Calvin, like Luther, believes is the only one possible, and which implies a negation of the value of human action in the work of salvation, as well as a general relativization of the material dimension (which has consequences for anthropology)? Before answering this question, we will examine the impact which these principles of Luthero-Calvinist thought have had on modern philosophy.

---

[55] Ibid., III.XII.8.
[56] Ibid., IV.XIV.26.

As examples, we will briefly mention Thomas Hobbes, Emmanuel Kant, Karl Marx, and Friedrich Nietzsche. I do not intend to set Luther or Calvin up as direct ancestors of these philosophers, who are largely worlds apart from the two reformers. Rather, I simply want to show how certain principles can lead to opposite consequences from those intended, since the premises of opposite extremes are often very similar.

CHAPTER 4

Concurrence Between God and Man in Modern Philosophy

THE PREMISES WHICH UNDERLIE Luther and Calvin's view are clear, although never explicitly stated: since God and man cannot be left to coexist on the decisive level, to avoid insulting the dignity of God, man must withdraw from this domain. For Luther, one consequence of this view is that a whole part of human life unfolds outside the sphere of salvation, although it must reflect this sphere. We will now endeavor to show how modern philosophy has drawn different conclusions from the same premises.

Hobbes (1588–1679):
The Relationship Between Men

Hobbes's anthropology is deeply pessimistic: "To speak impartially, both sayings are very true; That Man to Man is a kind of God; and that Man to Man is an arrant Wolfe. The first is true, if we compare Citizens amongst themselves; and the second, if we compare Cities."[1] Man cannot

---

[1] Hobbes, Dedication, "To the Right Honourable, William, Earle of Devonshire," of *De Cive: Philosophicall Rudiments Concerning Government and Society. Or, A Dissertation Concerning Man in his severall habitudes and respects, as the Member of a Society, first Secular, and than Sacred. Containing The Elements of Civill Politie in the Agreement*

live in peace without the tutelage of a powerful authority: "Hereby it is manifest that during the time men live without a common Power to keep them all in awe, they are in that condition which is called Warre; and such a warre, as is of every man, against every man."[2] Lacking such authority, man lives in perpetual fear, without security; and as a result, commerce, industry, navigation, transportation, culture, art, and the like are impossible.[3]

Gabriella Cotta suggests a parallel between Luther and Hobbes. To understand fallen man essentially in terms of opposition can lead, via the cultural influence diffused by the Reformation (more than by the direct influence of Luther on Hobbes, which is very unlikely), to the constitutive opposition of man, no longer against God, but against other men:

> One could say, therefore, that extreme Lutheran voluntarism is the last possible development of an ontology which is still founded on a theological position. In fact, it represented the culmination of a relationship between transcendence and immanence, constructed *a contrario* in relation to the being of a God utterly unknowable in his nature. Beyond that, one could only formulate an ontology

which it hath both with *Naturall and Divine Lawes* (printed by J. C. for R. Royston, at the Angel in Ivie-Lane, London, 1651).

[2] Hobbes, *Leviathan,* rev. student ed. (Cambridge: Cambridge University Press, 1997), ch. 13, p. 88.

[3] Cf. ibid., ch. 13, p. 89: "Whatsoever therefore is consequent to a time of Warre, where every man is Enemy to every man; the same is consequent to the time wherein men live without other security, than what their own strength, and their own invention, shall furnish them withall. In such condition there is no place for Industry; because the fruit thereof is uncertain: and consequently no Culture of the Earth; no Navigation, nor use of the commodities that may be imported by Sea; no commodious Building; no Instruments of moving and removing such things as require much force; no Knowledge of the face of the Earth; no account of Time; no Arts; no Letters; no Society; and which is worst of all, continual fear, and danger of violent death; And the life of man, solitary, poor, nasty, brutish, and short."

which was still voluntaristic, like that of Hobbes, but completely detached from all connection with transcendence and structured around man's being, in itself and for itself, apprehending it not in opposition to God, but in opposition to the other man. In both cases, the essence of the relationships is nothing other than will vs. opponent, utterly stripped of freedom. In my opinion, this fact constitutes an undeniable point of contact [between Luther and] Hobbesian anthropology.[4]

Kant (1724–1804):
The Relationship Between God and Man

Belief in God was fairly natural in the atmosphere in which Kant lived, and Kant undertakes to defend faith in God by opposing skepticism,[5] although he remains aloof from his

---

[4] "Si può dire, perciò, che l'estremo volontarismo luterano è l'ultimo sviluppo possibile di un'ontologia ancora fondata a partire da un assunto teologico. Essa, infatti, rappresentava l'esito finale di un rapporto fra trascendenza e immanenza costruito a contrario rispetto all'essere di un Dio del tutto inconoscibile in natura sua. Oltre non si poteva ipotizzare altro che un'ontologia ancora volontaristica, come quella hobbesiana, ma del tutto sciolta da ogni legame con la trascendenza, e strutturata intorno all'essere in sé e per sé dell'uomo, ormai colto nella sua opposizione non a Dio, ma all'altro uomo. In entrambi i casi l'essenza di questi non è altro che volontà/contro, del tutto priva di libertà. Questo fatto costituisce, a mio avviso, un indubbio punto di contatto con l'antropologia hobbesiana" (Cotta, *La nascita dell'individualismo politico,* 62).

[5] Thus, he criticizes Hume because he "gave himself over entirely to *scepticism,* having, as he believed, discovered that what had hitherto been regarded as reason was but an all-prevalent illusion infecting our faculty of knowledge" (Immanuel Kant, *Critique of Pure Reason,* B 128). He wants to combat "temptation either of abandoning itself to a sceptical despair, or of assuming an obstinate attitude, dogmatically committing itself to certain assertions" (ibid., B 434). Cf. also ibid., B 167–68; Kant, *Critique of Judgment,* trans. J. H. Bernard, Hafner Library of Classics 14 (New York: Hafner Publishing Co., 1951), §21, p. 76, and §40, p. 138.
    Cf. Patricia A. Crawford, "Kant and the Refutation of Scepticism," in *Actes du Congrès d'Ottawa sur Kant dans les traditions anglo-*

society's established religion.[6] The question of God, together with freedom and immortality, is for him one of the three great questions of philosophy, one of the three "unavoidable problems set by pure reason."[7] Although he clashes with Lutheran orthodoxy, he has nonetheless inherited certain Lutheran presuppositions.[8]

Here we will not examine Kant's attitude toward religion, but rather the impact which his view of our potential for knowing God's existence has on the relationship between God and man.

In the *Critique of Pure Reason*, Kant seems to be essentially questioning the possibility of speaking of God: "I maintain that all attempts to employ reason in theology in any merely speculative manner are altogether fruitless."[9] He is convinced that the traditional arguments in favor of the existence of

américaine et continentale tenu du 10 au 14 octobre 1974 (Ottawa: Editions de l'Université d'Ottawa, 1976), 344–49.

6 Kant proposes a new approach to religion in his famous work *Religion within the Limits of Reason Alone* (cf. for instance the English translation by Theodore M. Greene and Hoyt H. Hudson [La Salle, IL: Open Court Publishing, 1934; reprint, New York: Harper, Perennial, 1960]).

7 Introduction to *Critique of Pure Reason*, B 7; cf. also B 395, Kant's note, and B 826: "The ultimate aim to which the speculation of reason in its transcendental employment is directed concerns three objects: the freedom of the will, the immortality of the soul, and the existence of God." Cf. also the summary of the three postulates of pure practical reason in Kant, *Critique of Practical Reason*, AK V 132.

8 Cf. the two following works: Jürgen Eiben, *Von Luther zu Kant— Der deutsche Sonderweg in die Moderne: Eine soziologische Betrachtung* (Wiesbaden: Deutscher Universitätsverlag, 1989); Heinz W. Cassirer, *Grace and Law: St. Paul, Kant and the Hebrew Prophets* (Grand Rapids: Eerdmans, 1988). Neither of these two works adequately discusses the link with Luther (the first because it suffers from a certain superficiality, which the critics have pointed out, and the second because it does not directly treat Luther), but they are helpful in providing some idea of this link.

9 *Critique of Pure Reason*, B 664.

God were never really convincing to the general public and remained limited to small circles.[10]

Kant is not trying to exclude the existence of God; rather, he wants to speak of it accurately, by substituting true, effective arguments for false, counterproductive ones. In order to accomplish this goal, he begins by criticizing the traditional arguments for the existence of God. As far as he is concerned, there are three such arguments, the only ones which he acknowledges:[11] the physico-theological argument, the cosmological argument, and the ontological argument. I will not discuss his refutation of the ontological argument,[12] partly because I agree with him on this

---

[10] Cf. preface of the second edition of the *Critique of Pure Reason*, B XXXII. Kant clarifies that his accusation does not refer so much to the content transmitted by his predecessors, but to the fact that they do not give the general public the means of attaining it: "reserving the key to themselves, and communicating to the public their use only" (ibid.).

This sensitivity to the difficulties inherent in arguing about God appears from the precritical period on, cf. Immanuel Kant, *The One Possible Basis for a Demonstration of the Existence of God* (1763), trans. Gordon Treash, Janus Library (New York: Abaris Books, 1979), Foreword, 44–45: "Achievement of this goal, however, requires that one venture into the fathomless abyss of metaphysics. This is a dark ocean without coasts and without lighthouses, where one must begin like a mariner on a deserted ocean who, as soon as he steps on land somewhere, must test his passage. . . . This demonstration has, however, not yet been discovered—which has already been noted by others. What I provide here is only the basis for such a demonstration *[Beweisgrund]* the painstakingly assembled material for building."

[11] Cf. *Critique of Pure Reason*, B 618–19.

[12] The ontological argument argues that a necessary being exists necessarily. Being is here a predicate of the necessary being (in Kant's terms: in this context, I would speak rather of existence). But " '*Being*' is obviously not a real predicate; that is, it is not a concept of something which could be added to the concept of a thing" (*Critique of Pure Reason*, B 626. This argument is already found in *The One Possible Basis for a Demonstration of the Existence of God*, I.I.II,

point, but also because his refutation of the cosmological argument is the significant one in the context of our study. In order to understand his rejection of the cosmological argument, however, it will be useful to review briefly why he rejects the physico-theological argument.

The physico-theological argument reasons back from the world to its supreme cause, founded on a contemplative wonder before the order of the universe.[13] Despite his affinity for this argument,[14] Kant finds it inadequate. He maintains that at best, the argument can only culminate in a hypothesis, since the scope of our knowledge precludes a comprehensive approach, even in the physical order (for instance, we do not know all possible worlds).[15] In other words, the argument proceeds from the starting point of the beings which we know, seeking their cause. But in order

---

pp. 59–63). Furthermore, "Were we dealing with an object of the senses, we could not confound the existence of the thing with the mere concept of it" (*Critique of Pure Reason,* B 628). For Kant, it is here that the specific weakness of the ontological argument lies.

[13] Cf. *Critique of Pure Reason,* B 650: "This world presents to us so immeasurable a stage of variety, order, purposiveness, and beauty, as displayed alike in its infinite extent and in the unlimited divisibility of its parts, that even with such knowledge as our weak understanding can acquire of it, we are brought face to face with so many marvels immeasurably great, that all speech loses its force, all numbers their power to measure, our thoughts themselves all definiteness, and that our judgment of the whole resolves itself into an amazement which is speechless."

[14] Cf. ibid., B 651: "This proof always deserves to be mentioned with respect. It is the oldest, the clearest, and the most accordant with the common reason of mankind." Cf. similarly *Critique of Judging,* §91, 329.

[15] Cf. *Critique of Practical Reason,* AK V 139. *Critique of Judging* (§85, pp. 291–92) explains that what is being called into question is at once the limitation of our experience and the "qualitative leap" which must be made between the empirical chain and a being outside this chain. To wish to dominate this ensemble amounts to presuming ourselves omniscient.

to make a general survey of the question and find the universal cause, one would have to know all things.

The second argument is more profound than the first. Whereas the physico-theological argument presupposes exhaustive knowledge, the cosmological argument only "start[s] from experience which is purely indeterminate."[16] Instead of proceeding from the existence of this or that being, it proceeds from the fact that there is something, in general. The consideration of efficient causes is enhanced by a consideration of the relationship between the contingent and the necessary.[17]

Here we find a point which is of interest to our discussion. Kant criticizes the cosmological argument, because "the transcendental principle whereby from the contingent we infer a cause (. . .) is applicable only in the sensible world."[18] Consequently, empirical change can only lead back to a cause which is part of the world: "The necessary being must therefore be regarded as the highest member of the cosmical series."[19] Thus natural theology should be careful not to propose a God of the empirical world[20] (besides

---

16 *Critique of Pure Reason,* B 618.

17 Cf. the distinction which St. Thomas Aquinas makes between the second and third ways (Ia, q. 2, a. 3, corpus).

18 *Critique of Pure Reason,* B 637. This argument gives rise to another: "The inference to a first cause, from the impossibility of an infinite series of causes, given one after the other, in the sensible world. The principles of the employment of reason do not justify this conclusion even within the world of experience; still less beyond this world in a realm into which this series can never be extended" (*Critique of Pure Reason,* B 638).

19 Ibid., B 487. Cf. also ibid., B 664: "If the empirically valid law of causality is to lead to the original being, the latter must belong to the chain of objects of experience, and in that case it would, like all appearances, be itself again conditioned."

20 Cf. ibid., B 71: "In natural theology, in thinking an object [God], who not only can never be an object of intuition to us but cannot be an object of sensible intuition even to himself, we are careful to

the fact that such a God would hinder our liberty[21]). This difficulty in the relationship between the "necessary being" and the empirical world mutually affects both terms. Thus it impacts the empirical world as well: this world cannot be explained by a cause which does not belong to it, since a "hyperphysical" explanation is not adapted to a physical world.[22] Hence, it is evident that arguments like the cosmological argument (as well as the other "physical" arguments, i.e., the physico-theological argument and the ontological argument) can never come to an end.[23] Kant maintains that instead, a moral proof founded on practical necessities makes it possible to establish the existence of God.[24]

---

remove the conditions of time and space from his intuition—for all his knowledge must be intuition, and not *thought*, which always involves limitations. But with what right can we do this if we have previously made time and space forms of things in themselves, and such as would remain, as *a priori* conditions of the existence of things, even though the things themselves were removed? As conditions of all existence in general, they must also be conditions of the existence of God." This idea is already heralded in 1763, during Kant's precritical period, cf. *The One Possible Basis for a Demonstration of the Existence of God*, V.II.1, p. 149, where Kant makes the following criticism of the physico-theological proof: "What is most pernicious to the intent of physico-theology is that it considers the contingency of natural perfection as highly essential to the proof of a wise creator."

21 Cf. *Critique of Practical Reason*, AK V 100–101. Cf. also *Opus postumum*, Bundle I, 2, p. 206, AK XXI 19.

22 Cf. *Critique of Pure Reason*, B 800–801: "Order and purposiveness in nature must themselves be explained from natural grounds and according to natural laws; and the wildest hypotheses, if only they are physical, are here more tolerable than a hyperphysical hypothesis, such as the appeal to a divine Author, assumed simply in order that we may have an explanation. That would be a principle of ignava ratio." Cf. also *Of the Different Human Races*, AK II 440.

23 Cf. *Critique of Pure Reason*, B 769–70.

24 Cf. *Critique of Pure Reason*, B 856: "It is quite otherwise with *moral belief*. For here it is absolutely necessary that something must happen, namely, that I must in all points conform to the moral law. The end is here irrefragably established, and according to such insight as

The problem with Kant, then, lies in his inability to conceive of the relationship between two levels of being. Whatever the differences between the two thinkers (in particular, Luther does not share the Kantian criticism of causality), it was the same lack of a metaphysics of being which prevented Luther from seeing God and man any other way than in concurrence, and Kant from recognizing the classical arguments for the existence of God.

Kant's method initially attains its goal: the existence of God remains well established. But then its only remaining bastion, after the self-styled "definitive destruction" of the physical or metaphysical arguments, is a desire for morality, which would soon cease to be an argument. I have mentioned this topic not in order to address the whole of this issue, but to show that denying the possibility of relating the being of God and the being of man in a causal relationship between two different levels of being destroys most of the

---

I can have, there is only one possible condition under which this end can connect with all other ends, and thereby have practical validity, namely, that there be a God and a future world. I also know with complete certainty that no one can be acquainted with any other conditions which lead to the same unity of ends under the moral law. Since, therefore, the moral precept is at the same time my maxim (reason prescribing that it should be so), I inevitably believe in the existence of God and in a future life, and I am certain that nothing can shake this belief, since my moral principles would thereby be themselves overthrown, and I cannot disclaim them without becoming abhorrent in my own eyes." In fact, the moral level is even the only level on which God can be useful: "In order to have a religious value (the only value it needs to have, since it is not needed for the explanation of nature from a speculative standpoint) the concept of God must be the concept of a moral being" (*On the Failure of All Attempted Philosophical Theodicies* [1791], trans. Michel Despland, in Michel Despland, *Kant on History and Religion* [Montreal: McGill University Press; London: Queen's University Press, 1973], 284, Kant's note 1).

possibility for reasoning about the existence of God and, in the end, encourages atheism, or at least agnosticism.[25]

Marx (1818–1883):
The Relationship Between God and Man

As for Marx, we will merely refer to a commentary on Marx's atheism by an eminent specialist, Fr. Georges Cottier. Marx explicitly makes God man's rival:

> A being does not present itself as independent *(selbständig)* except insofar as it is its own master *(auf eigenen Füssen steht)* and it is not its own master except insofar as it owes its own existence *(Dasein)* to itself. A man who lives thanks to another is considered a dependent *(abhängig)* being. But I live completely dependent on the goodwill of another, when I owe him not only the sustaining of my life, but when he has also created *(geschaffen)* my life; when he is the source of my life and my life necessarily has this a foundation outside itself, when my life is not my own creation.[26]

---

[25] According to Kant, atheism is no stronger than the physico-theological, cosmological, or ontological arguments, since the sole conclusion which can be drawn from the debate for or against the existence of God is that it cannot possibly be resolved. Kant's transcendental theology makes it possible to eliminate from the notion of a supreme being everything "to free it from whatever, as belonging to mere appearance (anthropomorphism in its wider sense), is out of keeping with the supreme reality, and at the same time to dispose of all counter-assertions, whether *atheistic, deistic,* or *anthropomorphic.* Such critical treatment is, indeed, far from being difficult, inasmuch as the same grounds which have enabled us to demonstrate the inability of human reason to maintain the existence of such a being must also suffice to prove the invalidity of all counter-assertions" (*Critique of Pure Reason,* B 668–69).

But it still remains true that the criticism of the arguments for God's existence can also lead further than Kant thought.

[26] M.E.G.A. 42, pp. 138–40, quoted in Georges Cottier, *L'athéisme du jeune Marx: Ses origines hégéliennes* (Paris: Vrin, 1959), 342 [here translated into English].

After an investigation of Marx's philosophical background (Feuerbach and Hegel), Fr. Cottier identifies a problem which resembles Luther's:

> Being is univocal: hence, how is it possible to participate in the divine perfections without oneself being God or, conversely, attacking the unicity of the Most High? . . . Feuerbach's and Marx's humanism must be understood in this light; it opted for Man. In the place of a God whose magnitude derives from crushing man, it substitutes a man whose magnitude derives from casting out God. The Lutheran theology of sin and Marxist humanism constitute two explanations and two twin spiritualities.[27]

In fact, the premises are the same: God and man are on the same level of being, and what is granted to one must be taken away from the other. But where Luther chose God, Marx chose man.

Nietzsche (1844–1900): The Relationship Between God and Man

I do not think it is excessive to see an implicit acceptance of concurrence between God and man in some of Nietzsche's texts, such as the following: "that I may reveal my heart entirely unto you, my friends: If there were gods, how could I endure it to be no God! Therefore there are no Gods."[28]

The Dynamics of the Choice Between God and Man

As we have seen, the reformers create an opposition between God and man in order to exalt God. Catholics share this

---

27 Cottier, *L'athéisme du jeune Marx*, 344.
28 Friedrich Nietzsche, *Thus Spake Zarathustra*, book II, "In the Happy Isles," trans. Thomas Common, eBooks@Adelaide, 2004.

desire to exalt God, but I think that this goal would be better achieved using a different method, namely, by believing that God can and does make man his collaborator. The principles of the reformers' thought preclude seeing man as God's collaborator, and these predominantly theological principles have naturally resulted, as it were, in excluding God from the human sphere. If two terms are in opposition, one must choose which one of the two to eliminate, but either way, one is eliminated.

The tragedy of this logic of opposition is that it backfires on the affirmation of the glory of God; and in the same stroke, it turns on man as well, as the sequence of history (which obeys a whole set of factors) shows. For Luther, "God can only be everything, if man is nothing."[29] But man does not feel like nothing, and later would think it necessary to affirm himself against God. Fr. Sesboüé summarizes this process:

> The same line of thought leads Protestantism to exalt the absolute sovereignty of God (i.e., Calvin's *soli Deo gloria*). But this affirmation seems to be made at the expense of man, as though the lower man is, the more proportionally greater God is; as though uplifting man constitutes an attempt on divine glory. Is there not a certain dualism here, structured on a principle of rivalry? . . . But we are far-removed from Irenaeus' beautiful phrase: "The glory of God is man fully alive, and the life of man is the vision of

---

[29] "Dieu n'est tout que si l'homme n'est rien" (Chantraine, *Erasme et Luther,* 451). This ontological statement has a much more radical meaning than St. John of the Cross's mystical expressions *(Todo y nada),* and Luther's problem may be that he failed to distinguish between these levels of language.

God." Hence, understandably, such a unilateral goal was
deemed intolerable and historically gave birth to its opposite, i.e., the demand for a human autonomy which would
banish God.[30]

---

[30] "La même ligne de pensée amène le protestantisme à exalter la sou-
veraineté absolue de Dieu (c'est le *soli Deo gloria* de Calvin). Mais
cette affirmation semble se faire aux dépens de l'homme, comme si
Dieu pouvait être d'autant plus grand que l'homme est plus bas,
comme si toute élévation de l'homme devait porter atteinte à la
gloire divine. N'y a-t-il pas ici un certain dualisme, habité par un
schéma de rivalité? . . . Mais nous sommes loin du beau mot
d'Irénée: 'La gloire de Dieu c'est l'homme vivant, et la vie de
l'homme c'est la vision de Dieu.' On comprend dès lors qu'une visée
aussi unilatérale soit perçue comme insupportable et engendre his-
toriquement son contraire, c'est-à-dire la revendication d'une
autonomie de l'homme, qui exile Dieu" (Sesboüé, *Pour une théologie
oecuménique*, 184–85).

CHAPTER 5

The State of the Question in the Twentieth Century Outside Catholic–Lutheran Dialogue on Justification

IN THE PREVIOUS CHAPTERS, we verified that the concept of a systematic opposition between God and man is a current flowing deep within the thought of Luther and Calvin. We then showed the cultural impact of this current of thought.

Another question now arises: is contemporary Protestantism, which has often radically departed from the teachings of its founders, still influenced by this same mindset, whose origins by now are centuries old?

We will proceed with a twofold inquiry into Protestantism in the twentieth century: first, a study of texts which are not specifically consecrated to dialogue on justification; and second, a study of the dialogue between Catholics and Lutherans on justification.

This chapter will briefly examine two major Protestant theologians of the twentieth century: Karl Barth and Paul Tillich. To reach a broader view of present-day Protestantism, we will look at extracts from the responses of the Protestant churches to the BEM *(Baptism, Eucharist, and Ministry)*. Finally, we will read two documents from the dialogue between Catholics and the Reformed.

Karl Barth (1886–1968)

One of the masters of Protestant theology in the twentieth century, Karl Barth, asserts that all the points on which Catholicism and Protestantism differ are as nothing compared to the following: "I regard the *analogia entis* as the invention of Antichrist, and think that because of it one can not become Catholic. Whereupon I at the same time allow myself to regard all other possible reasons for not becoming Catholic, as shortsighted and lacking in seriousness."[1] It should be noted that he does not reject analogy as such: on the contrary, he considers it necessary, and his understanding of it is very close to St. Thomas's. First of all, he demonstrates a thorough grasp of the deadlock created by what Thomas calls univocity and equivocity:

> Does there exist a simple parity of content and meaning when we apply the same word to the creature on the one hand and to God's revelation and God on the other? . . . Obviously we cannot affirm this. . . . Ought we, then, to speak of a disparity of content and meaning when we apply a description to the creature on the one hand and to God's revelation and God on the other? . . . [Do words] mean something different from when we use them to describe the creature? . . . [U]nder the presupposition of a simple disparity, there cannot possibly be any question of the veracity of our knowledge of God.[2]

Next, he praises a theological solution which corresponds to that of St. Thomas:

---

[1] Karl Barth, *Church Dogmatics,* vol. 1, part 1: *The Doctrine of the Word of God,* trans. G. T. Thomson (Edinburgh: T&T Clark, 1955), x.

[2] Ibid., vol. 2, part 1: *The Doctrine of God,* trans. T. H. L. Parker et al., ed. G. W. Bromiley and T. F. Torrance (Edinburgh: T&T Clark, 1957), 224–25.

[T]he older theology accepted the concept of analogy to describe the fellowship [between the knower and the known]. By this term both the false thesis of parity and the equally false thesis of disparity were attacked and destroyed, but the elements of truth in both were revealed. It could therefore be claimed as the correct definition of the matter. . . . [T]he object itself—God's truth in His revelation as the basis of the veracity of our knowledge of God—does not leave us any option but to resort to this concept.[3]

Accordingly, he does not reject analogy as a measure of language; but on the other hand, he does reject the analogy of being.

Barth believes that in the wake of original sin, the only knowledge of God we have comes to us from Revelation. Consequently, theology must be founded on Scripture alone, and the only analogy possible is the *analogia fidei*, the analogy of faith.

What presuppositions underlie Barth's rejection of the analogy of being? First of all, he thinks that the analogy of being claims to know the essence of God, and worse, to know it through a philosophical approach: "We possess no analogy on the basis of which the nature and being of God as the Lord can be accessible to us."[4] This is certainly not St. Thomas's view: "because we cannot know what God is, but rather what He is not, we have no means for considering how God is, but rather how He is not."[5] Barth's misunderstanding derives from the fact that like Kant, he thinks that an analogical approach would make God the same kind of being as earthly beings, only elevated to an infinite

---

[3] Ibid., 225.
[4] Ibid., 75.
[5] Ia, q. 3, prologue. Of course, to know what God is not, already constitutes the beginning of knowledge of what he is: since God is not non-life, he is living. . . .

level: "But it is not the case that we have only to extend our idea of lord and lordship into the infinite and absolute and we will finally arrive at God the lord and His lordship."[6] He expresses the same concern in his interpretation of certain Fathers, that is, when Athanasius and Augustine say that God is good (or other attributes) in a different way from us: "If we could only be sure that this *nec ita* or *aliter*, this αλλως or ετερως, does not refer only to a superlative of unlikeness, but to a basic difference between God and the creature, and therefore between the divine being and creaturely views, concepts and words!"[7] What Barth is looking for in these texts is the affirmation that God is not on our level of being as its highest actualization, but on a different level altogether—which, in fact, he is. In rejecting a poorly understood analogy of being, Barth is really seeking the analogy of being, properly understood.

Pastor Henry Chavannes has very accurately concluded that the analogy which Barth attacks in St. Thomas does not really correspond with Thomas's position, but with that of Przywara, whom Barth thought to be a genuine representative of Thomism, but who was actually closer to Scotus and Suarez.[8] Thus, believing that he is criticizing St. Thomas, Barth actually rediscovers the latter's position on several points.[9] Besides, Chavannes adds, Barth cannot understand St. Thomas because "at this point, the idealist postulate is so self-evident for Karl Barth that he does not even suspect that people might have thought differently in the past."[10]

---

[6] Barth, *Church Dogmatics,* vol. 2, part 1, p. 75.

[7] Ibid., 222.

[8] Henry Chavannes, *L'analogie entre Dieu et le monde, selon saint Thomas d'Aquin et selon Karl Barth,* Cogitatio Fidei 42 (Paris: Cerf, 1969).

[9] Ibid., 278–79.

[10] "[L]e postulat idéaliste est à ce point pour Karl Barth une évidence qu'il ne soupçonne même pas qu'on ait pu penser différemment dans le passé" (ibid., 243).

Although Barth certainly rejects idealism, he cannot escape from it himself;[11] consequently, his mental universe is closed to comprehending an author such as Thomas Aquinas.

Paul Tillich (1886–1967)

A contemporary of Barth, Paul Tillich is another of the major thinkers within present-day Protestantism. My aim here is not to present the entirety of his work, but rather to pause on one specific point: the relationship between Catholicism and Protestantism at their deepest level.

Tillich does not believe that the proper method of discerning the relationship between Catholicism and Protestantism is to compare their doctrines one by one. For him, the relationship involves two religious attitudes (generally manifested in respect to sacred things), which have distinct, but complementary, approaches to everything: the Protestant principle and the Catholic Substance, with the prophet and the priest as their central figure. Each of the

---

[11] Cf. ibid., 210–11 [here translated from French]: "St. Thomas's doctrine is realist, in the sense that the knowing subject attains in the known object the being which it has in the nature of things. . . . When the known object is God, our knowledge has very specific limits. . . . Conversely, idealism makes the being of the known object depend in one way or another on the activity of the knowing subject. We should remember Kant's famous words: 'Up till now, it was admitted that all knowledge should be measured according to objects. . . . We should try instead . . . [to suppose] that objects should be measured according to our knowledge . . .' Without being Kantian, Barth operates in a post-Kantian universe and he uncritically accepts, as a self-evident truth, the dependence of the known object on the knowing subject, in the act of knowing which is natural to man. And this idea explains both his judgment on pre-critical thought, particularly that of St. Thomas, and his protests against natural theology. It is as though Barth had reasoned thus: all of man's natural knowledge implies a seizure of the known object by the knowing subject, a confiscation of the object by the subject. . . . If, then, man knows God according to the laws of our nature, his knowledge can only end in alienating God."

two attitudes may be found as much in Catholicism as in Protestantism's various confessional groups, of course with an emphasis on one of the attitudes.

The Protestant principle undermines the human aspect:

> It should be regarded as the Protestant principle that, in relation to God, God alone can act and that no human claim, especially no religious claim, no intellectual or moral or devotional "work," can reunite us with him.[12]

Catholicism adheres to that which is stable and visible (sacraments, places, institutions, texts, definitions). At heart, Protestantism certainly adheres to Scripture in a sacramental way, as well as to Baptism and the Lord's Supper at least (which in Tillich's view constitutes the Catholic dimension of Protestantism), but it embodies a sort of permanent distrust of all institutional regimentation.

This approach presents two points of interest for our study. First, Tillich recognizes that one cannot be content with comparing the scattered elements of Catholicism and Protestantism. Both must be grasped in their entirety.[13]

The second point of interest is Tillich's identification of the Protestant principle: namely, an inflexible refusal to be bound to human elements. This is a very profound—though certainly not exhaustive—aspect of Protestantism, evinced by the way Protestantism has evolved throughout its history.[14] But one should seek out the root of this atti-

---

[12] Paul Tillich, *Systematic Theology,* vol. 3: *Life and the Spirit, History and the Kingdom of God* (Chicago: University of Chicago, 1963), 224.

[13] Cf. Paul Tillich, "The Permanent Significance of the Catholic Church for Protestantism," *Protestant Digest* 3, no. 10 (1941): 23–31.

[14] Cf. Paul Tillich, *The Protestant Era* (Abridged), trans. James Luther Adams (Chicago: University of Chicago Press, 1957), 169: "The Reformation struggled against two ideologies, that is, against two ways of concealing the true human situation, namely, the Catholic and the humanistic ideology. Catholicism claims to offer a secure

tude, which I believe to be an inability to countenance the presence of the transcendent God in a created intermediary. It is this dynamic which precludes analogy.

Official Responses to the BEM

In 1982, the Commission on Faith and Order (the only commission of the World Council of Churches of which the Catholic Church is a member) published the document *Baptism, Eucharist, and Ministry* (commonly referred to as "BEM").[15] All of Faith and Order's member churches were invited to answer some questions regarding the content of this document, and almost all of them replied. These responses, collected by Max Thurian,[16] are a very valuable witness to the faith of diverse Christian communities concerning the points on which many of their traditional differences focus. We will examine the degree to which the

---

way of overcoming the separation of man from his divine ground through sacramental graces and ascetic exercises, the efficacy of which is guaranteed by the hierarchy and its sacramental powers. Humanism denies the perverted character of the human situation and tries to achieve essential humanity on the basis of human self-determination. Over against these two ideologies—the religious and the secular—Protestantism must insist upon the unveiled and realistic recognition of the perennial situation of man. Historical Protestantism, however, has not escaped the ideologizing of its own principle. Protestant orthodoxy and Protestant idealism represent the sacramental and the humanistic forms of the old ideologies. In both forms a 'man-made God' has been substituted for the true God, a God that is either inclosed in a set of doctrines or is believed to be accessible through morals and education. In the power of the Protestant principle, Protestantism must fight not only against other ideologies but also against its own."

15 Faith and Order, *Baptism, Eucharist, and Ministry* (Geneva: World Council of Churches, 1982).

16 Cf. Max Thurian, ed., *Churches Respond to BEM*, 6 vols. (Geneva: World Council of Churches, 1986–88). Abbreviated henceforth CRBEM, followed by the volume and page numbers (i.e., CRBEM III, 234).

responses of the different contemporary Protestant communities still express the presupposition which we have been unfolding: namely, the idea that upholding the participation of any human action in the gift of grace constitutes an offense to divine majesty.

Regarding ministry, the Lutheran Church of Hanover expresses the following concern: "Any notion according to which the witness (martyria) or proclamation (kerygma) of the truth is entrusted or given to certain members of God's people only (related to an authoritative or governmental function) misunderstands the immediate authoritative work of God through the gospel and thus deprives listeners to the word of the saving certainty."[17] In expressing its satisfaction with another aspect of the BEM, the Lutheran Church of Iceland manifests an identical point of view: "We agree with the argument of §33 that the preservation of the gospel does not depend on a certain structure, and that the Holy Spirit has often taken unusual measures when admonishing the church. It is necessary to keep in mind that the life of the church is entirely dependent on God and his initiative."[18]

The Evangelical (i.e., Protestant)[19] Church of the Rhineland explains that "only word and sacrament are the foundation of the church. For us the focus of unity is neither ministry nor minister, but only what Christ bestows

---

[17] Evangelical Lutheran Church of Hanover, in CRBEM IV, 53. Cf. also Evangelical Church of the Augsburg Confession (Austria), in CRBEM IV, 19: "The ordained ministry is made central to such an extent that the absolute authority of the Lord of the church is diminished."

[18] Evangelical Lutheran Church of Iceland, in CRBEM IV, 67.

[19] In German, an "Evangelical" church is a traditional Protestant church. This usage must not be confused with the American usage, which has also been imported into French, according to which an "Evangelical" church is a "free" or Pentecostal church, etc., and thus distinct from the traditional Protestant churches.

on us through their proclamation. Thus the making present (representation) and realization of Christ occurs in the exercise of the ministry. But the holders of office do not become Christ's representatives."[20] In fact, ministry and the Church as a whole have a passive role, according to the response given by the Evangelical Church in Baden: "Who is acting in the celebration of the eucharist: Christ or the church? . . . We are concerned that [the text of the BEM] does not adequately reflect our church's view that it is first and foremost Christ himself who is the giver, and the congregation who are receivers. While it is clear that the church as the body of Christ participates in his action in the eucharist, nevertheless it is still above all a receiving church."[21] In other words, Christ is present in his members, but "remains juxtaposed to the empirical church."[22]

The Salvation Army pushes this logic to an extreme in rejecting the celebration of any sacrament. It is therefore not surprising that its lengthy response reinforces the concerns which we have just seen expressed by more traditional Protestant churches: "We firmly reject the idea that any work or rite can accomplish what God has promised in response to faith"; "The text . . . fails to make clear the crucial distinction between the sign and the truth signified,

---

[20] Evangelical Church of the Rhineland, in CRBEM V, 85. Cf. also the response given by the East-German Methodists: "the 'sacramental' understanding of ministry (§§41, 53) . . . endangers the strong personality of the tie to Christ (according to Reformation theology). This personality is also damaged when clergy take the place of Christ as his 'representative' (§11 and repeatedly)" (Evangelical-Methodist Church: Central Conference in the German Democratic Republic, in CRBEM IV, 172).

[21] Evangelical Church in Baden, in CRBEM V, 46–47.

[22] Cf. Evangelical Church in Hesse and Nassau, in CRBEM IV, 129: "It is also very important for us to make a distinction between God's acting in Christ and the actions of the church. Even though Christ is present in his members, he remains juxtaposed to the empirical church."

between the shadow and the reality. It ascribes to the sacraments powers belonging to the Holy Spirit alone."[23]

The response of the Waldensian and Methodist Churches in Italy summarizes several elements of this standard Protestant position: "[C]hurch and ministries are at the service of God and his work of grace and cannot be presented as if they were proprietors, guarantors and dispensers of the grace of God."[24] We can highlight three elements here: ministries should not be (1) proprietors, (2) guarantors, or (3) dispensers of grace. Every Christian would willingly agree that the ministers of the Church are not proprietors of divine grace; and historical experience of abuses in ministry contributes to explaining the Waldensians' concern. We will not discuss here the possible role of ministers as guarantors.[25] Rather, we are primarily interested in the question of whether they can be dispensers of grace. The Message to the Churches of the Permanent Lutheran-Reformed Council of France about the BEM (sent as a common response, to which separate responses were attached) very specifically highlights this point: "We maintain, with BEM, the necessity of structures for all ecclesiastical life. We think, however, that the church and its ministries are never in themselves dispensers or sole purveyors of grace. Every activity of the church and ministries

---

[23] Salvation Army, in CRBEM IV, 235 and 254.

[24] Waldensian and Methodist Churches in Italy, in CRBEM II, 247.

[25] For instance, one would have to speak of the relationship between preaching the faith and the infallibility of the Church, or of the objective validity of the administration of the sacraments, which would be too much of a digression in this context. The reader can refer to two articles which I have already published on this question: "La primauté de Pierre," in Boris Bobrinskoy, Patrick Chauvet, et al., *Qu'ils soient un: L'oecuménisme dans le sillage du Père Marie-Joseph Le Guillou* (Paris: Éditions Parole et Silence, 2001), 75–104; and "L'infaillibilité du pape selon Jean de Saint-Thomas," *Nova et Vetera* 77, no. 1 (2002): 5–35.

has to be simply a means for the clear discernment of an activity which is God's alone."[26] The Protestant churches constantly reiterate that even if structures legitimately occur on an organizational level, they are not required for the validity of sacramental acts or for the nature of the Church: "Since Lutheran doctrine differentiates very carefully and concretely between the authority of the Lord who is himself present in the Supper and the authority of the ordained minister whom he authorizes to act, we cannot possibly make the validity of a celebration of the Lord's Supper depend on its being conducted by an ordained minister, even though, in practice, in the interests of 'due' order, we take great care to ensure that this is the case."[27] For the Federation of Swiss Protestant Churches, the overvaluation of ministry corresponds to an undervaluation of the action of the Holy Spirit.[28] In other words—the words of the response of the Presbyterian Church of Rwanda—

---

[26] Message of the Permanent Lutheran-Reformed Council of France, 1985, regarding the BEM, in CRBEM III, 144. Cf. also the Decision of the Synod of the Reformed Church of France, Strasbourg, 1985, in CRBEM III, 164: "We would be unable to accept that the church and ministers, whose calling is to serve God and the work of his grace, might seem to be dispensing or controlling that grace."

[27] North Elbian Evangelical Church, in CRBEM I, 50. As regards the specific form of ministry, the Lutheran churches, like the Swedish, Finnish, and Norwegian churches, whose ministers include bishops, priests, and deacons, maintain that this distinction is useful for good order, but not necessary (cf. Church of Sweden, in CRBEM II, 138; Church of Finland, in CRBEM III, 123; Church of Norway, in CRBEM II, 120).

[28] Cf. Federation of Swiss Protestant Churches, in CRBEM VI, 83: "Could it not be that the 'office' of the ministry acquires such a decisive role in relation to recognition of a celebration of the Lord's supper and to the unity of the church generally, because in the chapters on baptism and comments on the Lord's supper insufficient account has been taken of what the Holy Spirit does by word and proclamation to gather the people of God?"

ministry "should not be tied to human persons because the gifts of God are not tied to human beings."[29]

Despite the great diversity of the Protestant traditions mentioned (Lutheran, Reformed, Methodist, Salvation Army), a very widespread concern can be detected regarding forms of ministry and the recognized place of the sacraments, that the BEM's emphasis on ministry might imply an undervaluation of the action of God.

Once more, then, our question is as follows: in order to safeguard divine transcendence, is it clearly necessary to empty of their efficacy all the actions accomplished by men on behalf of a divine institution? The answer to this question involves presuppositions which none of the responses to the BEM mention, because no one has even guessed at their existence.

The Joint Catholic-Protestant Committee in France (1987) and Its Commentators

In 1987, the Joint Catholic-Protestant Committee in France tried to identify the fundamental difference between Catholics and Protestants[30] in order to overcome it.

The text is theological rather than philosophical, which somewhat limits its scope. But as a theological text, it deserves hearty approval: "The difference between us therefore does not concern the fact of the Church's instrumentality in the transmission of salvation, but the nature of this

---

[29] The context here is apostolic succession: "As regards apostolic succession, we consider that it should not be tied to human persons because the gifts of God are not tied to human beings" (Presbyterian Church of Rwanda, in CRBEM III, 184).

[30] The majority of whom were Reformed, for which reason we will not treat this text as though it were typical of dialogue between Catholics and Lutherans.

instrumentality: is the church sanctified in such a way as to become herself the sanctifying subject?"[31]

The Committee's text is illuminated by two studies, one Protestant (André Birmelé), and the other Catholic (Bernard Sesboüé). Both explicitly identify the question which we have been examining.

André Birmelé indicates that a feature which all the different obstacles to ecumenical dialogue have in common is the issue of cooperation:

> As regards ministries, one may note a collection of open questions (the relationship between particular ministry and universal priesthood, apostolic succession, the triple form of ministry, the sacramental and indelible character of ordination, papal ministry . . .). All these questions converge at one point: the concept of the minister ordained as God's cooperator. Protestant theology recognizes a similar cooperation, but simply as an instrument for the proclamation of the Word and the celebration of the sacraments. Catholic theology speaks of the participation of the ordained ministry in the priesthood of Christ (Vatican II, *LG* 10, *PO* 2), which enables the ordained minister to have a sanctifying action, especially within the Eucharistic celebration. The same set of problems appear regarding the reference to Sacred Scripture and the difficult question of the magisterium. What is the role of the church and her magisterium? Is the church sanctified by God to the point of being able to be the authorized and decisive interpreter of Scripture? In the same way, regarding marriage: does the church effectively cooperate with God in the sense that she must consider it her duty to

---

[31] "La divergence entre nous ne concerne donc pas le fait de l'instrumentalité de l'Église dans la transmission du salut, mais la nature de cette instrumentalité: l'Église est-elle sanctifiée de manière à devenir elle même sujet sanctifiant?" (Comité Mixte Catholique-Protestant de France, *Consensus oecuménique et différence fondamentale* [Paris: Le Centurion, 1987], no. 11, p. 20).

uphold fidelity to the Gospel by means of ecclesiastical
norms and to control the rupture of fidelity in a juridical
manner? The issue at stake in all these questions seems to me
to be quite simple. Is the church, particularly in her concrete
institutional form, sanctified by God to the point of becoming herself the subject of a sanctifying action? In what way
do the church and especially ministry and the ecclesial hierarchy cooperate with God in the salvation of men?[32]

He adds some clarifications intended to eliminate superficial misunderstandings:

> In order to avoid all misunderstandings, two things must
> be clarified. For the churches of the Reformation too, it is

---

[32] "À propos des ministères, on note un ensemble de questions
ouvertes (relation ministère particulier—sacerdoce universel, succession apostolique, triple forme du ministère, caractère sacramentel et
indélébile de l'ordination, ministère papal . . .). Toutes ces questions
convergent en un point: la notion du ministère ordonné coopérateur
de Dieu. La théologie protestante connaît pareille coopération, mais
elle est simplement instrumentale pour la proclamation de la Parole
et la célébration des sacrements. La théologie catholique parle de
participation du ministère ordonné au sacerdoce du Christ (Vatican
II, *LG* 10, *PO* 2) qui habilite le ministre ordonné à avoir, en particulier lors de la célébration eucharistique, un agir sanctifiant. La
même problématique apparaît à propos de la référence à l'Écriture
Sainte et de la difficile question du magistère. Quel est le rôle de
l'Église et de son magistère? L'Église est-elle sanctifiée par Dieu au
point de pouvoir être l'interprète autorisé et décisif de l'Écriture? De
même, à propos du mariage: l'Église est-elle coopératrice effective de
Dieu dans le sens qu'elle a à considérer comme étant de son devoir
d'appuyer la fidélité à l'Évangile au moyen de normes ecclésiastiques
et de contrôler la rupture de la fidélité de manière juridique? L'enjeu
de toutes ces questions me semble être simple. L'enjeu est la compréhension même de l'Église. L'Église et en particulier sa forme
institutionnelle concrète est-elle sanctifiée par Dieu au point de
devenir elle-même sujet d'un agir sanctifiant? De quelle manière
l'Église et en particulier le ministère et la hiérarchie ecclésiale
coopèrent-ils avec Dieu au salut des hommes?" (André Birmelé,
"Analyse protestante," in Comité Mixte Catholique-Protestant de
France, *Consensus oecuménique et différence fondamentale*, 38–39).

evident that the church, ministries, and all believers cooperate with God in the salvation of humanity. But this cooperation is the cooperation of receiving. God is the sole subject of a saving action. Moreover, it must be insisted upon that in Catholic theology, God is understood to be the first subject. The church does not claim to put herself in the place of God. She understands herself simply as an effective and efficacious cooperator. What is at stake here is not the church's cooperation in the work of God, but the way in which this cooperation is understood. We all think that the church is an instrument of salvation, but it is on the nature of this instrumentality that our disagreements arise.[33]

Although the positions are not as far apart as they seem, the difference identified here touches on the entirety of the themes of dialogue: "This difference, which may seem minimal and which is effectively quite small in comparison to the broad consensus, still has at the moment a separating character and seems to me to be the last source which indicates and explains the separating character of our differences."[34] Professor Birmelé deplores the fact that Catholic theologians relativize this question, since it is a foundational

---

[33] "Afin d'éviter tout malentendu, il faut bien préciser deux choses. Il est, aussi pour les Églises de la Réforme, évident que l'Église, les ministères et tous les croyants coopèrent avec Dieu au salut de l'humanité. Mais cette coopération est la coopération du recevoir. Dieu est le seul sujet d'un agir salvateur. Il faut, par ailleurs, insister sur le fait que dans la théologie catholique, il est entendu que Dieu reste le sujet premier. L'Église ne prétend pas se mettre à la place de Dieu. Elle se comprend simplement comme coopératrice effective et efficace. L'enjeu n'est pas la coopération de l'Église à l'oeuvre de Dieu, mais la manière dont cette coopération est comprise. Nous pensons tous que l'Église est instrument du salut, mais c'est sur la nature de cette instrumentalité que porte notre désaccord" (ibid., 39).

[34] "Cette différence qui peut sembler minime et qui est effectivement petite à côté de l'ample consensus, a pour le moment encore un caractère séparateur et me semble être la source dernière qui indique et explique le caractère séparateur de nos différences" (ibid.).

principle for the Reformation.[35] I warmly commend the diagnosis he presents.

Fr. Sesboüé brings up the same issue from the standpoint of causality:

> An important question thus remains to be clarified between us, not that of the "hierarchy of truths," but that of the "hierarchy of causes," or the ladder of causality. It requires us to renounce an over-simplified alternative between God and man, as though what is done by one must be taken away from the other. But does this not recall the way of understanding justification through grace, and the relationship between grace and graced freedom? Moreover, one can speak of cause in many ways. I have used the term "analogy"; do we not see the ghost of the famous question of the analogy of being, rising up beneath our feet?[36]

I entirely commend this diagnosis, which the author does not develop in this short text. In a later work, Fr. Sesboüé returns to the same topic, concluding that "the essential rift" between the Reformation and the Catholic Church "hinges on the conception of the relationship between God and man."[37] He

---

[35] Cf. ibid., 42–43.

[36] "Une importante question reste donc à clarifier entre nous, non pas celle de la 'hiérarchie des vérités,' mais celle de la 'hiérarchie des causes,' ou de l'échelle de la causalité. Elle nous demande de renoncer à une alternative trop simple entre Dieu et l'homme, comme si ce que ferait l'un devait être enlevé à l'autre. Mais ce point ne nous renvoie-t-il pas à la manière de comprendre la justification par la grâce? Et au rapport entre grâce et liberté graciée? D'autre part la cause se dit de plusieurs manières: j'ai employé le terme d'analogie; ne voyons-nous pas resurgir sous nos pieds le spectre de la fameuse questioin de l'analogie de l'être?" (Bernard Sesboüé, "Analyse catholique," in Comité Mixte Catholique-Protestant de France, *Consensus oecuménique et différence fondamentale,* 58). This text is taken up again in Sesboüé, *Pour une théologie oecuménique,* 165–68.

[37] "[L]e clivage essentiel tourne sur la conception du rapport de l'homme à Dieu" (Sesboüé, *Pour une théologie oecuménique,* 61).

extends his diagnosis to the central theme of the Reformation: "I think that the Protestant thematization of justification was not balanced enough. It is always afraid of giving too much to man and calling God's priority into question."[38] And this could be the level on which reconciliation can occur: "Together we must mine the deep logic which progresses from justification by faith to the mystery of the Church. Doubtless, it is there that the real chance of reconciling our separating differences is to be found."[39]

Towards a Common Understanding of the Church (1990)

In 1990, the International Commission for Catholic-Reformed Dialogue published the document *Towards a Common Understanding of the Church*.[40] After two chapters devoted respectively to history and to the confession of common faith, the third chapter explores the ministerial and instrumental role of the Church.

Discussing the notion of sacrament, the text speaks of the Church as an instrument, while underlining the dependent nature of an instrument:

> The terms "sacrament" and "sign" imply coherence and continuity between diverse moments of the economy of salvation; they designate the Church at once as the place of

---

[38] "j'estime que la thématisation protestante de la justification n'est pas suffisamment équilibrée. Elle a toujours peur de trop donner à l'homme et de mettre en cause la priorité de Dieu" (ibid., 65).

[39] "nous avons ensemble à creuser la logique profonde qui va de la justification par la foi au mystère de l'Église. C'est sans doute là que réside la vraie chance de réconciliation de nos divergences séparatrices." (ibid., 183).

[40] International Commission for Catholic-Reformed Dialogue, *Towards a Common Understanding of the Church*, in *Information Service*, English ed., 74 (1990): 91–125. References will quote the paragraph numbers, which are the same for all editions.

presence and the place of distance; and they depict the
Church as instrument and ministry of the unique mediation of Christ. Of this unique mediation the Church is the
servant, but never its source or its mistress.[41]

A little further on, the text addresses mutual concerns
about the instrumentality of the Church:

> The Reformed commonly allege that Catholics appropriate
> to the Church the role proper to Christ. Roman Catholics,
> for their part, commonly accuse the Reformed of holding
> the Church apart from the work of salvation and of giving
> up the assurance that Christ is truly present and acting in
> his Church. Both these views are caricatures, but they can
> help to focus attention on genuine underlying differences
> of perspective of which the themes of creatura verbi and
> sacramentum gratiae serve as symbols.[42]

The text invites Catholics not to caricaturize Reformed
ecclesiology by claiming that it denies the presence of
Christ in his Church. In fact, we have seen that Calvin
emphasizes the importance of the Church. Nevertheless,
another issue remains to be addressed: not that of Christ's
action in his Church, but that of the real value of the action
of men (other than Christ) in the Church. From a Catholic
point of view, one must certainly be careful not to place all
the weight on men, as though the Church could subsist
without its Head, Christ. The text thus draws attention to
the "genuine underlying differences," but does not identify
them clearly, because it fails to identify their root.

---

[41] Ibid., no. 107. Cf. also no. 108: "The Church is an instrument in
Christ's hands because it carries out, through the preaching of the
Word, the administration of the sacraments and the oversight of
communities, a ministry entirely dependent on the Lord, just like a
tool in the hand of a worker."

[42] Ibid., no. 112.

We have shown that the systematic opposition which the Reformers set between divine action and human action is still widespread within contemporary Protestantism, and that this opposition has sometimes been identified on the theological level, but not on the underlying philosophical level.

We are now in a position to address this same question using texts specifically devoted to dialogue between Catholics and Lutherans on justification.

CHAPTER 6
Catholic–Lutheran Dialogue on Justification

FROM THE OUTSET, the principles behind the relationship of causes have been at the heart of the Lutheran understanding of justification. Now, however, an agreement has been reached on justification. How does this agreement relate to both systems of philosophical thought? In order to answer this question, we will begin with a history of the dialogue between Catholics and Lutherans on justification.

The Prehistory of Dialogue

Article 4 of the Augsburg Confession (read aloud before Emperor Charles V in 1530) discloses the traditional Lutheran understanding of faith:

> Also they teach that men cannot be justified before God by their own strength, merits, or works, but are freely justified for Christ's sake, through faith, when they believe that they are received into favor, and that their sins are forgiven for Christ's sake, who, by His death, has made satisfaction for our sins. This faith God imputes for righteousness in His sight. Rom. 3 and 4.[1]

---

[1] http://users.frii.com/gosplow/augsburg.html#augs-004.

The expression of the Catholic position is fundamentally no different. The sixth session of the Council of Trent (1547) clarifies this basic point: "If anyone says that, without divine grace through Jesus Christ, one can be justified before God by one's own works, whether they be done by one's own natural powers or through the teaching of the Law, *anathema sit.*"[2] The next canons add that grace is necessary essentially, not just to achieve greater facility,[3] and that the grace of justification cannot be obtained by human effort.[4]

The Council of Trent, then, laid the foundations for agreement a long time ago. It remains to be seen how an intention with a common basis can be understood in common, where misunderstandings have persisted through centuries of theological work.

A short history of ecumenical dialogue on justification illustrates both the basic consensus and mutual misunderstandings.

Repeated Attempts at Ecumenical Consensus on Justification

The idea that we have finally reached a common understanding of justification has continually resurfaced since 1972, with the first document of the Lutheran-Roman Catholic International Commission for Dialogue:

---

[2] Cf. Council of Trent, *Decree on Justification,* Canon 1, Denz. 1551, CF 1951.

[3] Cf. ibid., Canon 2, Denz. 1552: "If anyone says that divine grace is given through Jesus Christ only in order that one may more easily live justly and merit eternal life, as if by one's free will without grace one could do both, although with great difficulty, *anathema sit.*"

[4] Cf. ibid., Canon 3, Denz. 1553; "If anyone says that without the prevenient inspiration of the Holy Spirit and without his help one can believe, hope and love or be repentant, as is required, so that the grace of justification be bestowed upon one, *anathema sit.*"

Out of the question about the center of the gospel, arises the question of how the two sides understand justification. At this point the traditional polemical disagreements were especially sharply defined. Today, however, a far-reaching consensus is developing in the interpretation of justification. Catholic theologians also emphasize in reference to justification that God's gift of salvation for the believer is unconditional as far as human accomplishments are concerned.[5]

Optimism soared, to the point of seeing the document as a common basis which could thenceforth be used to address other questions: "A broad consensus emerges in the doctrine of justification, which was decisively important for the Reformation: it is solely by grace and by faith in Christ's saving work and not because of any merit in us that we are accepted by God and receive the Holy Spirit who renews our hearts and equips us for and calls us to good works."[6] This analysis is especially significant here since it occurs in a list of points of consensus, followed by a list of points which remain to be discussed (namely, the number of the sacraments, the papacy, the episcopal structure of the Church, the Magisterium, and the dogmas proclaimed after 1530).

Was This First Consensus Understood In Similar Ways?

Nevertheless, after the initial enthusiastic recognition of agreement, some wondered whether the consensus was so obvious. This was the question which the United States Joint Group for Lutheran-Catholic dialogue asked in 1985:

---

5 Joint Lutheran/Roman Catholic Study Commission, "The Gospel and the Church" (also called the Malta Report, 1972),no. 26 in *Lutheran World* XIX/3, 1972, 263.

6 Joint Lutheran/Roman Catholic Study Commission, "All Under One Christ" (1980), in *Facing Unity*, no. 14.

The Malta Report of the International Lutheran/Catholic Study Commission said in the course of a short section on the doctrine that "today . . . a far-reaching consensus is developing in the interpretation of justification." But a further treatment of the subject and its implications is needed. The present relationship between the Catholic and Lutheran traditions calls for a greater clarity about the way to understand and speak of justification than has yet been achieved in official discussions, for the good news of God's justifying action in Jesus Christ stands at the center of Christian faith and life.[7]

It is not surprising, then, that this inadequately settled issue was resurrected in the 1993 common text: "Catholics ask whether the Lutheran understanding of justification does not diminish the reality of the church; Lutherans ask whether the Catholic understanding of church does not obscure the gospel as the doctrine of justification explicates it."[8] This is an accurate identification of the link between one's conception of justification and one's conception of the Church as a whole. The document also noted that "the fact that the Reformation doctrine of justification and its emphasis on the unconditionality of the gift of salvation has at times been understood as questioning the necessity of the ordained ministry and the legitimacy of its institutional, ecclesial form calls for an even more pointed rejoinder."[9] An initial inquiry, however, reveals that this idea is mistaken:

---

[7] United States Joint Group for Lutheran-Catholic Dialogue, *Justification by Faith,* ed. T. George Anderson, T. Austin Murphy, and Joseph A. Burgess, Lutherans and Catholics in Dialogue 7 (Minneapolis: Augsburg Publishing House, 1985), 15, Introduction, no. 2.

[8] Joint Lutheran/Roman Catholic Study Commission, "Church and Justification" (1993), no. 166 in *Information Service* 86, 1994/ii–iii, 159.

[9] Ibid., no. 184. See the similar comment made about the episcopal ministry in no. 192. See the commission's general remarks in "The Gospel and the Church," no. 29: "According to Lutheran

[T]he Lutheran Reformation knows no such ecclesiological consequence of the doctrine of justification. There is no contradiction between the doctrine of justification and the idea of an ordained ministry instituted by God and necessary for the church. Quite the opposite. . . . Lutheran orthodoxy taught that the triune God is "the primary efficient cause" of the church and that the church's ministry is the "efficient cause which God uses to gather his church."[10]

The Faculty of Göttingen's statement of position provides an example of the relative lack of understanding which could still persist nearly twenty years after the first "consensus."

The Faculty of Göttingen (1991)

In 1991, the Göttingen Faculty of Evangelical (Lutheran) Theology published a work as one faculty, questioning what it considered to be a superficial or immature ecumenical agreement on a number of points. The Faculty points out that the doctrine of justification is the key to understanding the relationship between God and man: "The doctrine of justification is not just one dogmatic article among others, but the theological formulation of the event which marks the center of the Christian faith. . . . That is so because justification is the truth about the relationship of God and man; that is, in the event of justification God is

---

understanding, and on the basis of the confession of justification, all traditions and institutions of the church are subject to the criterion which asks whether they are enablers of the proper proclamation of the gospel and do not obscure the unconditional character of the gift of salvation. It follows that the rites and orders of the church are not to be imposed as conditions for salvation, but are valid only as the free unfolding of the obedience of faith."

10 "Church and Justification," no. 185. The quotation at the end of this text is from Johann Gerhard, *Loci theologici,* XXII.V, 37.40.

truly God, and man truly man—standing before God."[11]
Failure to understand man's relation to God in this way
entails a whole sequence of concrete consequences:

> That means nothing but that man in doing this and living
> this way wants to establish himself, and that in the realm of
> ethics and religion he wants to be his own creator, instead
> of recognizing that God alone is the Creator from whom
> man can do nothing but accept himself and all things.
> Such resistance to one's own creatureliness and dependence
> upon God necessarily leads to concrete ethical failure.[12]

Man is utterly passive before God.[13] The Faculty adds that
this central point gives rise to a particular way of thinking.[14]

Applying these principles to particulars, the Faculty
questions a certain way of understanding the efficacity of
the sacraments: "The church is precluded from generating
sacraments since it lacks the authority to unite physical elements with the efficacy of grace."[15] Through the sacraments, particularly the Mass, the Catholic Church arro-
gates to herself an illegitimate participation in salvation.[16]

---

[11] Theological Faculty, Georgia Augusta University, Göttingen, "An
Opinion on the Condemnations of the Reformation Era", *Lutheran
Quarterly* 5, no. 1 (1991): 15.

[12] Ibid., 16.

[13] "That God's saving deed occurs 'purely by grace' means that man
can be a recipient only and is thus totally passive" (ibid., 27).

[14] "To this 'center' there is not necessarily a certain 'mode of expression' attached, but there is a certain 'structure of thinking' which
defines the 'emphases' of the doctrine of justification" (ibid., 22).

[15] Theological Faculty, Georgia Augusta University, Göttingen, "An
Opinion on the Condemnations of the Reformation Era", *Lutheran
Quarterly* 5, no. 3 (1991): 338.

[16] Cf. ibid., 356–57: "The notion of sacramental pre-representation of
the sacrifice on the cross, taken as a sacrifice in itself, assigns to the
church a role to which it is not entitled. Thereby, in the form of its
office defined centrally on the basis of this function as priesthood, it
transposes the one-time event into the present and above all, when

This can even lead to profound misgivings on the nature of the Catholic Church as Church:

> [W]hat always and wherever it exists, *makes* the church the church and Christians Christians, that is what they explicitly confess and what defines their self-understanding as church—the gospel of Christ, who justifies by grace alone and by faith alone. Through nothing else the Roman Catholic Church too, is a Christian church. But in essential elements of her doctrine and her institutional form it stands in conflict with the gospel which makes it a church.[17]

Whatever importance ought to be accorded to a declaration such as Göttingen's, it shows at least that the question of justification directly relates to man's role in his salvation and that this question impacts the status of the whole Church.

The *Joint Declaration* of 1999

This situation seems to have cleared up in 1999.[18] The *Joint Declaration on the Doctrine of Justification*, published in

on its part it is active in making sacrifice, it, in fact, achieves participation in the work of atonement itself, however much its dependence on the historical starting-point is emphasized. . . . The facts that the crucifixion happened just once and that it is sufficient for salvation forbid such participation as illegitimate blurring of the permanent stance of Christ over against the church. That is especially clear with respect to the statement that 'the church enters into the sacramentally present, unrepeatable sacrifice of the cross.' "

17 Theological Faculty, Georgia Augusta University, Göttingen, "An Opinion on the Condemnations of the Reformation Era", *Lutheran Quarterly* 5, no. 4 (1991): 507–8. Nevertheless, it should be mentioned that the Faculty agrees that the Catholic Church is Church, and then adds, as though giving an important nuance to its statement, the text quoted here.

18 The text of the Joint Declaration on the Doctrine of Justification (JDDJ) is published in *Joint Declaration on the Doctrine of Justification: The Lutheran World Federation and the Roman Catholic Church* (Grand Rapids: W.B. Eerdmans Publishing Co., 2000). I will quote it from this edition, following the paragraph numbers in the Declaration. The

1997, was ratified on October 31, 1999, by the Lutheran World Federation (representing more than three quarters of the Lutherans in the world[19]) and the Catholic Church. This *Joint Declaration* established that "it becomes clear that the earlier mutual doctrinal condemnations do not apply to the teaching of the dialogue partners as presented in the Joint Declaration."[20] The question is thus resolved at a deep level, and an old misunderstanding vanishes. Still, Catholics and Lutherans had really been in agreement on this point from the very beginning, although they had apparently never understood each other. In particular, this backdrop of agreement did not prevent a whole series of differences in other elements of faith and Christian life from springing up in the past. This principle must now be applied to all other areas.

The *Declaration* does not definitively elucidate all the points which still await resolution: "Based on the consensus reached, continued dialogue is required specifically on the issues mentioned especially in the Joint Declaration itself (JD 43) as requiring further clarification, in order to reach full church communion, a unity in diversity, in which remaining differences would be 'reconciled' and no longer have a divisive force."[21] Certain differences appear con-

---

Catholic Church published its official response in 1998 [text available at http://www.lutheranworld.org/Special_Events/LWF-1999-Official_Documents.html]. Finally, a common statement of June 11, 1999, intended as an annex to the JDDJ, was published.

[19] According to the calculations of the Ecumenical Institute of Strasbourg, published in *Lutheran World Federation* 4/98, the LWF's favorable response, given on June 9, 1998, represents the agreement of 78.5% of the total Lutheran members of the World Lutheran Federation, while the responses of more than 10% were not known, which does not necessarily mean that they would be negative.

[20] Common statement 2.

[21] Common statement 3. Cf. also JDDJ 5: "[This declaration] does not cover all that either church teaches about justification; it does

cerning themes such as the regeneration of the sinner (in what sense can one say that the justified remain sinners?),[22] assurance of salvation,[23] and the way in which the role of works is understood.[24] On all these points, a consensus of sorts is explicitly perceived in different ways. Other questions which have traditionally set the two conceptions of justification at odds must still be addressed in themselves, "questions of varying importance which need further clarification. These include, among other topics, the relationship between the Word of God and church doctrine, as well as ecclesiology, authority in the church, ministry, the sacraments, and the relation between justification and social ethics."[25] We have more or less reached the point which Birmelé had already identified in 1986: "It seems that the essential stumbling-block in today's Lutheran-Catholic dialogue is the ecclesiological consequences of the agreement on justification."[26] But there is a notable difference: we have now attained a real consensus on justification.[27] Our next task is to discern together the significance of this consensus for the whole Church.

---

encompass a consensus on basis truths of the doctrine of justification and shows that the remaining differences in its explication are no longer the occasion for doctrinal condemnations."

[22] Cf. JDDJ 22–31.

[23] Cf. JDDJ 34–36.

[24] Cf. JDDJ 37–38.

[25] JDDJ 43.

[26] "Il semble que les conséquences ecclésiologiques de l'accord sur la justification soient le problème essentiel du dialogue luthéro-catholique actuel" (Birmelé, *Le Salut en Jésus-Christ*, 124–25).

[27] Birmelé too recognizes this noteworthy evolution, but with an optimism which I only partially share: "The definitive breakthrough in the JDDJ is that the fundamental difference no longer stands in the way of consensus. It was separatory, but has lost its separating character" (André Birmelé, *La communion ecclésiale: Progrès oecuméniques et enjeux méthodologiques*, Cogitatio Fidei 218 [Paris: Cerf; 2000] 253).

Numerous Protestant theologians have criticized the incomplete aspect of the *Declaration*. Eberhard Jüngel maintains that the somewhat reticent text is no different from the definition which the Council of Trent had specifically opposed to the Reformers,[28] and hence he finds it difficult to understand why the Lutherans would renounce the source of their identity. In 1998, about 160 German-speaking Protestant theologians[29] criticized the declaration in two statements of position,[30] and a slightly smaller group took up the criticism again in 1999.[31] In their 1998 text, these theologians express a concern that the centrality of justification not be minimized: "The 'Joint Declaration on the Doctrine of Justification' (JDDJ) should not be viewed as a dis-

---

[28] Eberhard Jüngel, *Das Evangelium von der Rechtfertigung des Gottlosen als Zentrum des christlichen Glaubens: Eine theologische Studie in ökumenischer Absicht* (Tübingen: Mohr Siebeck, 1998), xii: "Ich erwähne das alles, um die Enttäuschung verstandlich zu machen, die mich beim genaueren Studium jener so vielverspechenden Gemeinsamen Erklärung erfaßte. Hier waren nach meinem Urteil jedenfalls auf lutherischer Seite gerade keine soliden theologischen Fundamente 'zur Überwindung der Kirchenspaltung' gelegt worden . . . Gewiß, in diesem Text steht mancherlei, was die evangelischen Kirchen und die römisch-katholische Kirche gemeinsam sagen können. Aber dassind Aussagen, die sich fast durchweg im Horizont und auf dem Niveau des Rechtfertigungsdekretes bewegen, das die römisch-katholische Kirche auf dem Konzil von Trient anno 1547 aufgrund der, vor allem aber gegen die Rechtfertigungslehre der Reformatoren verabschiedet hatte."

[29] Eberhard Jüngel is not among them, but the promoters of the Göttingen text are.

[30] Original text: "Votum der Hochschullehrer zur 'Gemeinsamen Erklärung zur Rechtfertigungslehre' vom Januar 1998," *Materialdienst des Konfessionskundlichen Instituts Bensheim*, no. 2 (1998): 33–35. I am not aware of any translation into English.

[31] "Stellungnahme theologischer Hochschullehrer zur geplanten Unterzeichnung der Gemeinsamen Offiziellen Feststellung zur Rechtfertigungslehre," in *Materialdienst des Konfessionskundlichen Instituts Bensheim*, no. 6 (1999): 114–15. There is no known English translation of this statement.

cussion of one detail of theology; it has to do with the foundation and entirety, the article 'concerning which nothing can be yielded or abandoned' (Luther, Articles of Schmalkald) and with which the Church stands or falls."[32] Then they point out that no consensus, or an inadequate consensus, was obtained on points such as faith and assurance of salvation, good works, Law and the Gospel, and justification as the criterion for the teaching and life of the Church.[33] A clear sign of this lack of consensus, according to them, on a point which they consider pivotal and which demands resolution, is that "[a]s a result, nothing has been obtained for communal participation in the Lord's supper."[34] Adopting Jüngel's major concern, they conclude that obviously the

---

32 "In der 'Gemeinsamen Erklärung zur Rechtfertigungslehre' (GE) kann es folglich nicht um einen Einzelaspekt der Theologie gehen, vielmehr geht es um das Grundlegende und Ganze, um den Artikel, von dem man 'nichts weichen oder nachgeben' kann (Luther, Schmalkaldische Artikel), mit dem die Kirche steht und fällt" ("Votum der Hochschullehrer," §1, 33). "Votum der Hochschullehrer zur 'Gemeinsamen Erklärung zur Rechtfertigungslehre' vom Januar 1998," *Materialdienst des Konfessionskundlichen Instituts Bensheim,* no. 2 (1998): 33–35.

33 "Votum der Hochschullehrer," §2, 33: "Kein Konsens wurde erreicht über die für die lutherischen Kirchen entscheidende Einsicht, dass die Rechtfertigung allein aus Gnaden nur dann recht verkündigt wird, wenn dabei zur Geltung kommt, dass der allein aus Gnade am Sünder handelnde Gott 1. allein durch sein Wort und durch die diesem Wort gemäss gereichten Sakramente (CA 7) den Sünder rechtfertigt und 2. der Sünder allein durch den Glauben gerecht wird. Kein Konsens wurde erreicht über die für die reformatorischen Kirchen entscheidende Einsicht, dass Glaube Heilsgewissheit ist. Kein Konsens wurde erreicht über das Sündersein des Gerechtfertigten. Kein Konsens wurde erreicht über die Bedeutung der guten Werke für das Heil. Ein nur unzureichender Konsens wurde erreicht über das Verhältnis von Gesetz und Evangelium...Kein Konsens wurde erreicht über die Funktion der Rechtfertigungslehre als Kriterium für Lehre und Leben der Kirche."

34 "für die Abendmahlsgemeinschaft ist folglich auch nichts gewonnen" (ibid., §5, 33).

Catholic Church does not consider justification to be the sole criterion for the teaching and life of the Church.[35] The 1999 text begins by expressing disappointment that the issues mentioned the preceding year had had no effect.[36] Above all, it deplores the fact that the points on which complete agreement is still lacking were not settled before reaching an agreement on the central point:

> The JDDJ certainly recognizes that a supplementary study of numerous theological questions—including the doctrine of justification itself—is necessary. But the clarifications of fundamental points which can be expected from this future study should have been reached *before* a common recognition could have been responsibly signed.[37]

Finally, on the points where agreement was reached, the meaning of the texts was not Protestant: "The JDDJ does take up some Lutheran formulae, such as the '*simul justus et peccator*' or 'by faith alone,' but it interprets them in a Roman Catholic way, against their Protestant meaning."[38]

---

[35] Cf. ibid: "Daran zeigt sich einerseits, was es heißt, dass die römisch-katholische Kirche neben der Rechtfertigungslehre noch andere Kriterien für Leben und Lehre der Kirche vertritt (§18)."

[36] Cf. "Stellungnahme theologischer Hochschullehrer," §1, 114: "Keiner dieser Kritikpunkte ist durch die GOF wirklich entkräftet worden."

[37] "In der GOF wird die Tatsache anerkannt, dass eine Weiterarbeit an zahlreichen theologischen Fragen—einschließlich der Rechtfertigungslehre selbst—notwendig ist. Aber die von dieser Künftigen Arbeit erhofften Klärungen in Grundfragen müssten erreicht sein, *bevor* eine Gemeinsame Feststellung verantwortlicherweise unterzeichnet werden kann" ("Stellungnahme theologischer Hochschullehrer," §2, 114).

[38] "Die GOF nimmt zwar einige lutherische Formeln, z.B. das 'simul justus et peccator' oder das 'allein durch Glauben' auf, interpretiert sie jedoch gegen ihre reformatorische Bedeutung in römisch-katholischen Sinn" ("Stellungnahme theologischer Hochschullehrer," §3, 114). "Stellungnahme theologischer Hochschullehrer zur geplanten Unterzeichnung der Gemeinsamen Offiziellen Feststellung zur Rechtfertigungslehre," in *Materialdienst des Konfessionskundlichen Instituts Bensheim*, no. 6 (1999): 114–15. There is no known English translation of this statement.

Assessing Dialogue and the Consensus on Justification

To summarize, in the question of justification, there are elements both of agreement, that is, that it is God alone who saves by his grace, and of disagreement, that is, concerning the personal and ecclesial condition of the justified man. Although the protracted dialogue leading to the *Declaration* has enabled us to take a large step forward, it has left certain questions unresolved.

Some theologians recognize where the fundamental difference might be located. The American Catholic theologian Carl Peter is an excellent example:

> There are, as I see it, genuine differences between Lutheran and Roman Catholic members of the dialogue when it comes to assessing creaturely mediation and cooperation in the ways in which Christ's grace reaches human beings. Two different approaches are taken—motivated at least in part by diverse hopes and fears. Lutherans have a fear that the truth of Christ's unique mediation will be compromised and hope to avoid this by criticizing any function, form of worship or piety, office or person that looks like a pretender in this context. Roman Catholics fear that Christ's unique mediation will thus be made needlessly fruitless and hope to avoid this by stressing the truth of the manifold cooperation to which that mediation gives rise as his grace is communicated to those in need of it. I suspect that we are dealing here with what ecumenists today might call a fundamental difference. I doubt that it will ever be completely eliminated.[39]

(Later he asks if it is necessary to eliminate this difference in order to achieve unity). Similarly, the Lutheran André

---

[39] Carl J. Peter, "A Moment of Truth for Lutheran-Catholic Dialogue," *Origins* 17, no. 31 (1988): 541.

Birmelé points out this fundamental difference within the very *Declaration* itself, adding that it is difficult to identify this difference precisely:

> Finally, the JDDJ exemplifies the difficulty of naming the fundamental difference and summarizing it in a dogmatic statement. Given our way of introducing it, one could say that this difference lies in the understanding of the human being before God and the conception of justification which flows therefrom. One could also say that these approaches are only the result of different understandings of God, or different understandings of the human being, without, conversely, excluding the possibility that these different understandings of God or of the human being could be the result of different choices regarding justification. This game could go on indefinitely, going around in circles without reaching a satisfactory solution. The fundamental difference cannot be captured and summarized in a theological statement.[40]

Professor Birmelé is right: it is difficult to identify the fundamental difference from a theological standpoint. But perhaps the difficulty is caused precisely by limiting oneself to the theological level.

We should keep in mind that Luther's problem is no problem at all for the theological tradition illustrated

---

[40] "La DCJ montre enfin la difficulté de nommer la différence fondamentale et de la résumer en une affirmation dogmatique. Au vu de notre manière de l'introduire, on pourrait affirmer qu'elle réside dans la compréhension de l'être humain devant Dieu et de la conception de la justification qui en découle. On pourrait aussi dire que ces approches ne sont que la conséquence de compréhensions différentes de Dieu, ou de conceptions différentes de l'être humain, sans exclure, inversement, que ces compréhensions différentes de Dieu ou de l'être humain soient la conséquence de choix différents à propos de la justification. On pourrait indéfiniment poursuivre ce jeu qui fait tourner en rond sans proposer une solution satisfaisante. La différence fondamentale ne se laisse pas fixer et résumer en une affirmation théologique" (Birmelé, *La communion ecclésiale,* 253).

notably by St. Thomas Aquinas. Unlike Luther, St. Thomas consciously includes metaphysics in his reflection, so that he is able to avoid a theological impasse. The metaphysical dimension of this question should be highlighted, in order to help resolve the problems which remain after the *Declaration*, and promote a common understanding of them.

CHAPTER 7

Perspectives on Divine Majesty in Two Different Metaphysical Systems

HAVING REACHED THE END of our historical presentation of the Reformation's implicit understanding of the relationship between God and man, we will now summarize the relationship between two metaphysical systems.

Systems Oriented Toward Safeguarding Divine Transcendence

Gerhard Hennig summarizes Luther's reaction to the claim that human actions have some significance: "If God does not do everything, then the Word does not do everything, and if the Word does not do everything, then faith does not receive everything."[1] Protestant difficulties with accepting the Sacrament-Church of Vatican II[2] illustrate the same attitude: "To reflect on the sacramentality of the Church is not common in Lutheran theology. The Church-Sacrament association immediately wakes the suspicion that a potential

---

[1] "Weil Gott nicht alles tut, darum tut das Wort nicht alles, und weil das Wort nicht alles tut, darum empfängt der Glaube nicht alles" (Hennig, *Cajetan und Luther*, 52).

[2] Cf. *LG* 1 and *GS* 42.

inadmissible intermediary is being thrust between the justifying God and the believing man."[3]

To summarize the Catholic view on man's relationship with God, Cajetan likes to quote Dionysius the Areopagite: "there is nothing more divine than being made a cooperator with God."[4] This formula summarizes the Catholic understanding of redemption, but for Lutherans, it elicits the anxiety that Catholics might feel so thoroughly ransomed as to become the owners of a grace which they can dispose of without ever having to give thanks again.[5] May this fear serve as a warning to us. . . .

St. Thomas linked theology to metaphysics; Luther explicitly rejected metaphysics, but simply ends up creating

---

[3] "Réfléchir à la sacramentalité de l'Église n'est pas chose courante dans la théologie luthérienne. L'association Église-sacrament éveille immédiatement le soupçon d'un éventuel intermédiaire inadmissible entre le Dieu justifiant et l'homme croyant" (Birmelé, *Le Salut en Jésus-Christ,* 238). Cf. also Günther Gassman, "Kirche als Sakrament, Zeichen und Werkzeug. Die Rezeption dieser eccklesiologischen Perspektive in der ökumenische Diskussion," in *Die Sakramentalität der Kirche in der ökumenischen Diskussion* (Paderborn: éd. Johann Adam Möhler Institut, 1983), 171–201; Eberhard Jüngel, "Die Kirche als Sakrament?", in *ZTK* 80 (1983): 432–57; Comité Mixte Catholique-Protestante de France, *Consensus oecuménique et différence fondamentale,* no. 13, p. 22; Sesboüé, *Pour une théologie oecuménique,* 163–65.

[4] "[I]ta ad dignitatem membri christi pertinet ut cooperetur capiti suo ad acquirendam aeternam vitam. 'omnium enim divinissimum est,' inquit diony. ca. 3 cele. hier. 'dei cooperatorem fieri'" (Cajetan, *De fide et operibus adversus Lutheranos,* cap. IX). The same quotation from Dionysius is found in *In Summ. Theol.,* Ia, q. 44, a. 4, no. IV. The phrase in question has several variants; see P. Chevallier, *Dionysiaca: Recueil donnant l'ensemble des traductions latines des ouvrages attribués au Denys de l'Aréopage,* vol. 2 (Paris: Desclée de Brouwer, 1950), 791.

[5] Cf. Paul O'Callaghan, *Fides Christi: The Justification Debate* (Dublin: Four Court Press, 1997), 219. The author points out that the theology of created grace, which gave rise to this fear, actually signifies for St. Thomas "the transcendence and unconditioned quality of God's gracious self-giving" (223).

another metaphysics from this rejection. Yet both had the same intention: to safeguard the transcendence of God.[6]

6 In "placing Luther in a system," I am implying that there are others who could be ranked with him. In this regard, one could mention that the areas in which Biel is the least favorable to St. Thomas (based on the frequency of the citations and the way in which he evaluates them) are anthropology, the coherence between faith and reason, the analogy between God and the cosmos, and the questions regarding justification: i.e., contrition, grace, and merit (cf. Farthing, *Thomas Aquinas and Gabriel Biel*, 13, 192–93). Among the five main gaps in Biel's knowledge of St. Thomas, Farthing cites exemplarism, the doctrine of participation, analogical preaching, and ecclesiology (ibid., 29, 102). But these are key elements of St. Thomas's theology, especially concerning the relationship between God and man. And as in Luther, the result is manifested in relation to sacramental causality: "Thomas's notion of a restricted 'instrumental' and 'dispositive' causality finds no place in a doctrine that admits no causal medium, properly speaking, between the giver and the recipient of grace" (ibid., 107); "For the most part, Biel's voluminous citations from Thomas's works have the effect of presenting Thomas's thought in a very favorable light. The major exception to this is Biel's treatment of Thomas's doctrine of sacramental causality. Although he presents Thomas's opinion fully and fairly, Biel seems to fear that to regard sacraments as dispositive causes of grace is to cast aspersions upon the exclusively saving power of God himself" (ibid., 147). From this there flows a certain conception of the link between the sacraments and justification: ". . . for the primary importance of the sacraments—especially baptism, the eucharist, and penance—lies in their role as the means by which justifying grace impinges on the sinner's predicament. From the standpoint of an analysis of the religious roots of the Protestant schism, Biel's frequently maladroit handling of Thomas's teaching on these points is of considerable importance" (ibid., 148). Farthing manifests the centrality of this question: "It is hardly an exaggeration to say that in Germany, at least, the crisis initially had its roots in certain late medieval developments with respect to the doctrine of justification. Once the flame was ignited, a broad range of issues came up for criticism and reformulation. But the original spark came from an encounter with the semi-Pelagian tendencies that were at work at several points in the theological ambiguity of the late medieval period. The controversy over indulgences, for instance, carried an explosive potential that it would not have had except for the urgency of its implications for a number of issues related to the question of man's justification before God—faith and works, merit

This common intention has laid the foundations for dialogue, but in the meantime we have two different systems to deal with. Luther can be ranked with other thinkers, some of whom are notably Muslims:

> To insist as we have done on the necessity of creation to explain the existence of the universe, on the one hand; and on the exclusion of all creaturely participation from creating causality, on the other hand—is this not to deny the creature all real causality? Some have done this: the Arab philosophers commenting on Aristotle, like Averrhoës, or those simply concerned not to make any attempt on the transcendence of God as the Koran teaches it, like Malebranche in the sphere of Christian philosophy. This is the temptation which must be surmounted by any philosophy which tries to ponder the ways in which God relates to the creature: the disproportion can only be perceived as infinite, which tends to reduce the creature to nothing—unless, conversely, a vivid sense of the latter's reality leads to its separation from a God isolated in his transcendence, unknowable, useless, and finally nonexistent. Firmly grounded in the conjunction found in the Bible and Christian Tradition between wonderment before the beauties of creation and exclusive adoration of the Creator, between the vocation of creatures to glorify the Creator and the love which leads the Creator to magnify them, the theologian, and with him the Christian philosopher, must seek in the very transcendence of the Creator the source of the dignity of created being, of reality, and of the efficacy of creatures' acts. The relationship of created causality to creating causality is a privileged locus for this search.[7]

---

and charity, free will and grace. Nowhere is this pattern seen more clearly than in Gabriel Biel's soteriology and Martin Luther's response to it" (ibid., 150).

[7] "Insister, comme nous l'avons fait, sur la nécessité de la création pour expliquer que l'univers soit, d'une part; sur l'exclusion de toute participation de la créature à la causalité créatrice, d'autre part, n'est-ce pas refuser à la créature toute causalité réelle? D'aucuns l'ont fait:

Fr. Sertillanges highlights the same principles which Fr. Nicolas outlines regarding Creation, but with respect to predestination, and thus in the context of the relationship between grace and human action.[8]

---

les Philosophes arabes, commentateurs d'Aristote, comme Averroès, ou simplement soucieux de ne porter aucune atteinte à la transcendance de Dieu, telle que l'enseigne le Coran; dans l'aire de la philosophie chrétienne, un Malebranche. C'est la tentation que doit surmonter toute philosophie qui s'efforce de réfléchir sur les rapports de Dieu avec la créature: la disproportion ne peut être perçue que comme infinie, ce qui incline à réduire à rien la créature. À moins que le vif sentiment de la réalité de celle-ci ne conduise au contraire à la séparer d'un Dieu isolé dans sa transcendance, inconnaissable, inutile et finalement inexistant. Fermement appuyés sur la conjonction dans la Bible et dans la Tradition chrétienne, de l'émerveillement devant les beautés de la création et de l'adoration exclusive du Créature; de la vocation des créatures à glorifier le Créateur et de l'amour qui presse le Créateur à les magnifier, le théologien et avec lui le Philosophe chrétien se doivent de chercher dans la transcendance même du Créateur la source de la dignité du créé, de la réalité et de l'efficacité de son agir. Le rapport de la causalité créée à la causalité créatrice est un lieu privilégié de cette recherche" (Nicolas, "L'origine première des choses," 195–96).

8 Cf. Sertillanges, appendix "Prédestination," 324–25 [here translated from French]: "In the order of power—indeed, in any order—nothing is reduced into actuality without the intervention of the first in that order: God the author of nature, or God in the supernatural. . . . Whatever man causes is the same that God causes; whatever God causes is the same that man causes. St. Thomas constantly speaks like this, and he criticizes those who 'have drawn a distinction between that which flows from grace, and that which flows from free will, as if the same thing cannot come from both' (Ia, q. 23, a. 5). Here it is not a question of sharing, but of subordination; it is a matter of the necessary housing of the created in the uncreated, of the finite in the infinite and of all forms of being in Being. God is the cause of being as being: this formula, when properly understood, resolves everything. But who really understands it! Who can weigh its consequences! Everywhere we see nothing but men in a desperate struggle to find a compromise between man and God, to give much to God, and little to man, believing that in this way they are keeping their distance, that they are maintaining proportions, whereas the proportion of the created to the uncreated is incommensurable: everything that is from us and remains fully in us still makes no addition, and

The Theological Impact
of Lutheran "Metaphysics"

Fr. Congar, whose well-known ecumenical work is substantial and full of conviction, identified one of Protestantism's specific problems as "Elimination of the reality 'Church' as a constitutive element of the covenant relationship."[9] Perhaps this study has helped to clarify the meaning of this comment, which would seem unjust if it were understood as meaning that Protestantism denies the reality of the Church as such. It expresses a dynamic which, while affirming the importance of the Church, actually diminishes its role through a radical relativization of all human dimension on the religious level. This is what Gabriella Cotta admirably summarizes in her philosophical analysis:

> In approaching the Reformer's thought, one is immediately confronted with the constant use of a criterion, mental but especially intellectual—whose effects are found as much on the theoretical as on the practical level—which guides and influences the entirety of his work. This element, omnipresent to the point of becoming a veritable methodology,

---

> does not count at all, so to speak, before the Supreme Cause. To make anything count which comes from man, from the act of man, or from the merit of man, in concurrence with God, without being primarily from God, fully from God, from God as from an independent source, is blasphemy. An unconscious blasphemy, certainly, which does not qualify its authors; but blasphemy nonetheless, as regards accurate metaphysics and the right attitude towards God. How much more inspired is St. Augustine's perfect expression: 'In recompensing our merits, God only crowns his gifts.'"

[9] Yves Congar, *Tradition and traditions: An Historical and a Theological Essay* (New York: Macmillan, 1966, 463). He adds the question: "is Scripture the only divinely instituted means to unite us to God? The Catholic answers that the Church, united with Scripture, enters as a unique element, willed by God, into the establishment of man's relationship with God" (ibid., 482).

even though it does find its deepest motivations in the never-pacified agony to reaffirm the absolute dependence of all created things—and of man primarily—in relation to divine omnipotence, actually has (. . .) a very definite philosophical origin. We can identify these mechanics—which answered the Reformer's chief demand for a radicalized distance between God and man—as the attempt to eliminate from the entire life of faith and the spirit, whether one's own or another's, from private action as from public action, all form of mediation between transcendence and immanence. Where this goal might be difficult to achieve—with respect to the roles of Christ and the Church—the Reformer (. . .) deeply transforms the traditional roles.[10]

Fr. Tillard makes the same observation in strictly theological terms:

It seems to me . . . that justification is still an issue, but now in a different form. . . . Is the Church external to justification?

------

[10] "Accostandosi al pensiero del Riformatore ci s'imbatte immediatamente nell'uso costante di un criterio, mentale ma soprattutto intellettuale—i cui effetti sono riscontrabili sia a livello teorico sia practico–, che guida e influenza il complesso della sua opera. Tale elemento, ricorrente tanto da divenire una vera e propria meteodologia, pur trovando certamente le sue motivazioni profonde in un'ansia, mai placata, di riaffermare l'assoluta dipendenza di tutto il creato—e in primo luogo dell'uomo—dall'onnipotenza divina, tuttavia ha, come vedremo, una sua ben precisa origine filosofica. Possiamo ricondurre questo meccanismo—utilizzato dal Riformatore per rispondere alla sua esigenza primaria di radicalizzazione della distanza dell'uomo da Dio—al tentativo di eliminare, dall'intera vita della fede e della mente, propria e altrui, e dall'agire, sia privato sia pubblico, ogni forma di mediazione fra trascendenza e immanenza. Laddove questa operazione non sia suscettibile di essere portata a totale compimento—nel ruolo di Christo e della chiesa—il Riformatore, come vedremo, ne trasforma profondamente i ruoli tradizionali" (Cotta, *La nascita dell'individualismo politico*, 12–13).

A study of the theological discussions which underlie current
ecumenical dialogues, even at the highest level, shows that
here, two viewpoints confront each other, and the point at
which they touch is the exact point at which our divisions are
born. . . . In fact, whereas *Catholic* traditions (in the broad
sense of the term) ordinarily perceive the realities of the world
of grace in an inclusive way (grasping *both* God *and* man at
once, while maintaining a hierarchy between the two), *Protes-*
tant traditions (in the broad sense of the term) most often see
these realities in an exclusive way (*either* God *or* man, trans-
forming the transcendence of the first into unicity).[11]

Fr. Tillard extends his recognition of this difference by
exploring the meaning of justification: "What is it to be justified, saved, by the transcendent grace of God? The event of
Salvation cannot be reduced to the forgiveness of sin, the
non-attribution of fault, nor even a pure and simple individual divine adoptive filiation."[12] He explains that justification
implies communion and that according to this view, ministry
must be understood as an integral part of salvation; moreover, this ministry must actively render Christ present.[13] The

---

[11] "Il nous semble . . . que la question de la justification continue de se
poser, mais cette fois sous une forme nouvelle. . . . L'Église est-elle
extérieure à la justification? L'étude des discussions théologiques
appuyant les dialogues oecuméniques en cours, même au plus haut
niveau, montre qu'ici deux visions s'affrontent, et qu'elles touchent
au point précis où naissent nos divisions. . . . Alors, en effet, que les
traditions *catholiques* (au sens large du terme) envisagent d'ordinaire
les réalités du monde de la grâce d'une façon inclusive (saisissant à la
fois *et* Dieu *et* l'homme, tout en maintenant une hiérarchie entre
l'un et l'autre), les traditions *protestantes* (au sens large du terme) les
voient le plus souvent d'une façon exclusive (ou Dieu ou l'homme,
en transformant la transcendance du premier en unicité)" (Jean-
Marie R. Tillard, "Vers une nouvelle problématique de la 'justification,'" *Irénikon* 55 [1982]: 186).
[12] Ibid., 190.
[13] Ibid., 190–91.

category of instrument, applied to the Church or to ministry, simply clothes the neo-testamentary category of service.[14] The tendency to sever Christ from his ecclesial body
is opposed to the ecclesiology of communion (which is at
the heart of the "Tillardian" vision of ecumenism) and the
theology of the Incarnation.[15]

Metaphysics in Conformity With the Gospel

Is it a scandalous intrusion of philosophy into the domain
of faith to propose an approach to theology starting from
metaphysics? First of all, no one can avoid philosophical
presuppositions, and the more seriously the theologian
takes them, the more he is free of them.

Furthermore, St. Thomas's use of metaphysics makes it
possible to account for Scripture. In fact, do not the
Gospels show us Christ sending forth his disciples to
accomplish the works of salvation? This is what Cajetan's
1518 commentary on Luther's theology seems to indicate:

> The church does not do this on human authority but on
> the authority of God which is granted to it by the privilege
> *Quodcumque solveris.* Peter, as Christ's vicar and minister,
> acts on the authority of Christ, Nor is it surprising that he
> can free people from the punishment that is due to them
> by Christ's command, to which inner repentance obliges
> them and which is necessary for salvation, since he can free
> people from guilt, which goes beyond punishment to such
> a degree that the Jews said, "Who can forgive sins except

---

[14] Cf. Jean-Marie R. Tillard, in *Grundkonsens-Grunddifferenz: Studie
des Straßburger Instituts für ökumenische Forschung, Ergebnisse und
Dokumente,* ed. André Birmelé and Harding Meyer (Frankfurt: Otto
Lembeck Verlag; Paderborn: Bonifatius Verlag, 1992), 275.

[15] Cf. Tillard, "Vers une nouvelle problématique," 194.

God alone?" A priest, absolves from guilt and remits the sins of his penitents ministerially in line with Christ's saying, "If you remit anyone's sins, they are remitted."[16]

Where another metaphysics would obscure the Gospels, therefore, this metaphysics provides the basis for a peaceable understanding of the relationship between causalities, as expressed in the Gospels and in the life of the Church.

Without mentioning philosophy, the American Anglican (Episcopalian) theologian Russell R. Reno says exactly the same thing as Cajetan. He mentions an issue which arises within dialogue with American Lutherans, who criticize the importance which Anglicans accord to human gestures such as the imposition of hands in ordination:

> We ought to be careful, for the requirement of laying on of hands would seem to be exactly the sort of condition God chooses in Christ and for us. The scandalous worldly features of the tradition of apostolical succession, the physical act of laying on of hands, echoes the much more scandalously worldly and physical features of Christ's obedience. Further, if we chuckle at the notion that God might use a bishop's hands to ensure the survival of his people, then we may all too easily chuckle when the gospel places demands upon our hands—to feed the hungry and clothe

---

[16] "Nec hoc facit ecclesia humana sed divina authoritate sibi concessa ex privilegio *Quodcunque solveris* [Mt 16:19]: Petrus enim ut vicarius, et minister christi agit auctoritate christi. Nec mirum si potest absolvere a pena debita ex precepto christi, et ad quam obligat interior penitentia, et que est de necessitate salutis, quia potest absolvere a culpa: que tantum excedit penam ut iudei dixerint: *Quis potest peccata dimittere, nisi solus deus?* [Mk 2:7] Sacerdos enim ministerialiter absolvit a culpa et remittit peccata confitentium sibi, dicente christo: *Quorum remiseritis peccata, remittuntur eis.* [Jn 20:23]" (Cajetan, opusculae of 1518, in my edition, §IV.11; translation from the original Latin text by Fr. Simon Tugwell, OP).

the naked. Will we not dodge these gospel imperatives with
some self-serving line about how God does not establish
conditions, does not call human hands into action to do
his work? Far, then, from corrupting the evangelical purity
of the gospel, the requirement of historical succession is an
intensification of the penetrating power of the gospel.[17]

For the exegete who seeks to avoid fundamentalism,
reliance on the Bible presupposes the principles which we
have just outlined. The Christian understanding of Revelation presupposes that man can be an instrument of God.
Otherwise, one would be faced with the following alternative: is Scripture only the Word of God (with which fundamentalist Christians, like fundamentalist Muslims, would
agree, and for similar reasons: Islam's implicit metaphysical
framework similarly reduces human action) or only a
human word (which is the tendency of liberal theology)?
Vatican II eliminates the necessity for this choice precisely
by understanding man as an instrument: "To compose the
sacred books, God chose certain men who, all the while he
employed them in this task, made full use of their powers
and faculties so that, though he acted in them and by them,
it was as true authors that they consigned to writing whatever he wanted written, and no more."[18] All Protestant exegesis which seeks to avoid both fundamentalism and liberalism more or less unconsciously presupposes this principle,
which is actually a metaphysical one. It could make a good
starting point for dialogue.

---

[17] Russell R. Reno, "The Evangelical Significance of the Historic Epis-
copate," in *Inhabiting Unity: Theological Perspectives on the Proposed
Lutheran-Episcopal Concordat*, ed. Ephraim Radner and Russell R.
Reno (Grand Rapids: Eerdmans, 1995), 90.
[18] *DV* 11.

These few examples show that metaphysics is not necessarily a foreign body which marginalizes the Bible in theology. On the contrary, it can be an important means of understanding the Bible and integrating it into a comprehensive vision of existence.

Conclusion

IF WE TRACE THE ESSENTIALS of Catholic ecumenical dialogue back to the Second Vatican Council (without forgetting its precursors, which actually span several centuries), we can divide it into two phases. The first stage of dialogue placed an emphasis on seeking out common points between Christians. This approach was, and obviously remains, indispensable, allowing for rapid rapprochement. Nevertheless, experience has shown its inadequacy, giving rise to the question, if we are so close, what still distinguishes us? Or rather: if we have reached an agreement on this or that, in which aspects are we still different? During the past quarter-century, therefore, dialogue has begun to cultivate a search for "fundamental differences." The search for differences could not get under way before the discovery of common points had pacified old bitterness and highlighted what is already common to Christians of different communities. Once the desire for unity had gained admittance, the search for differences became a necessary instrument for the furthering of unity: how can one overcome differences of which one is unaware? Identifying differences gives us a roadmap for the ecumenical journey, a list of obstacles to overcome on the road toward unity.

The intention of this book is to suggest that among the various possible fundamental differences, the philosophical factor should be kept in mind.

In Part I, we reflected on the very meaning of the word "dialogue." Before undertaking any activity, it is wise to question oneself on what one is about to do. We did not examine the goal of ecumenical dialogue—a difficult question which I intend to address in another work—but the way in which it unfolds. Ecumenists are well aware that it is not enough, for example, to compare the positions of two Christian confessions on a particular point. Each point must be situated within the context of two complex systems, in which each element is joined to all the other elements of theology, culture, worldview, common and individual history, and so on. Our era has developed principles for understanding the relationship between systems, in the culturally dominant domain of the natural sciences. These principles are directly developed and explained not by scientists, but by philosophers of science (who describe and influence the work of scientists). We have therefore studied three leading expositors of this subject—Popper, Kuhn, Feyerabend—in order to formulate their understanding of the dialogue between systems. The salient feature of this concept is the great difficulty in choosing between systems: each system answers its own questions, which cannot be directly transposed into another system, and it is not unusual for different approaches to subsist side by side on account of their respective strong points. These principles, which were not primarily developed from a theological perspective, are also employed in ecumenical and interreligious dialogue, more or less consciously or explicitly, by theologians nourished in the techno-scientific culture. But scientific knowledge and theological knowledge are not comparable in all respects, especially because of revelation.

This is a significant fact, and it deserves to be pointed out for its own sake. Ecumenical dialogue cannot indiscriminately apply principles of dialogue which do not entirely correspond to its object. The problems with the "incommensurability" of scientific theories do not occur in the same way in theology. Scientific systems can be incommensurable on account of the limitations of human understanding; divine knowledge is not limited, and by his revelation God lifts us above our limitations, although without totally eliminating them.

If Revelation is the source of the difference between the two domains, it does not directly explain their relationship. To do so requires philosophical distinctions. The fact that these philosophical distinctions are not familiar to scientists and theologians does not help to clarify the relationship between the different areas of knowledge, and contributes to the unconscious encroaching of one area upon another. This affects the very identity, and thereby the whole content, of dialogue.

In Part II, I proposed that ecumenical dialogue should take into consideration the philosophical dimension which lies at the heart of the Reformation. This is an unusual approach, since Luther banished philosophy in his campaign to reject Scholasticism, and the philosophical dimension has been ignored in dialogue between Catholics and Protestants. I think that this silence is one of the reasons that certain lingering differences, like those which are mentioned in the 1999 *Joint Declaration on the Doctrine of Justification*, are difficult to grasp theologically. Even points of unity are harder to understand communally if the interpretive presuppositions are unconsciously different.

Not being outside time and culture, Luther was not immune to the philosophy which permeated his formation. In the deep recesses of his mind was a univocal idea of being

which came to him from a globally Scotist heritage, assimi-
lated all the more poorly for being unconscious (which
would lead him to developments foreign to Scotus himself).
In perceiving God and man univocally as beings of the same
kind, the Reformer was led to see their actions in terms of
concurrence. In fact, when one and the same action is per-
formed by two beings at the same level, since neither of the
two can accomplish it 100 percent, they mutually over-
shadow each other: "second causes obscure first causes."[1]
Under such conditions, it was necessary to exclude human
action from the realm of salvation in order to safeguard
divine majesty, at the risk of leaving man his autonomy in
"profane" life. Calvin would inherit these philosophical presuppositions from Luther's great theological themes. These
principles of thought remain surprisingly present in contemporary Protestantism (see the responses to the BEM),
although considerably distanced from Scotist influence.

Luther and Calvin's premises in this area were shared by
modern philosophers, who have drawn opposite conclusions
therefrom, thinking that it is necessary to complete the
process by eliminating God as a rival of man (Feuerbach,
Marx, Nietzsche). A similar evolution is to be feared in certain strains of Christology: there is a risk of exaggeratedly
emphasizing one of the two natures of Christ, because certain presuppositions make it difficult to envision their unity.

---

[1] "[D]ie secundae causae obscurant primas" (Luther, *Tischreden* 5227,
1540; the Latin text seems strange because the first word of this bilin-
gual text is German); LW 54, 400, translated: "Secondary causes
obscure the first cause," which is not precise. In the context, which
has an Augustinian tone, Luther is pondering the danger of focusing
all one's attention on creation and forgetting divine action in it
("God is in the creature, operates in it and creates. But we do not pay
enough attention to this, and we engage ourselves in searching out
second and philosophical causes. With such an approach, we will
never properly learn the article of creation," ibid. [here translated
from French]); but the expression betrays a more general mindset.

Nevertheless, according to St. Thomas Aquinas's point of view, neither of these oppositions is necessary. One and the same action can be simultaneously 100 percent the work of God and 100 percent the work of man, because God and man are two beings on different levels. Such a view of cooperation between divine and human action is presupposed in the interpretation of Scripture. Whoever does not want to have to choose between fundamentalism (every Scriptural text is directly the Word of God) or a kind of liberalism (the Bible is only a human word) must recognize that Scripture is entirely a divine work and entirely a human work, on two different levels. In the redaction of Scripture, as in the life of the Church, God acts through human action. In this respect, the part of Protestant exegesis which implicitly accepts such a view remains distinct from certain philosophical presuppositions held by the Reformation, in order to better serve the latter's intent.

A metaphysical consideration of being makes it clear that man does not work in concurrence with God. Far from imposing itself on the Word of God, this metaphysics lets us take into consideration the whole history of salvation, in which God acts for men, through the action of men, mindful that we are men: "God provides according to his condition. Now, man's condition is such that he is brought to grasp the spiritual and intelligible naturally through the senses."[2] The Incarnation is the supreme sign of a divine-human mode of action, which is perpetuated in another way in the Body of Christ. It is because he could recognize the action of God in man that St. Thomas Aquinas saw the community of the disciples of Jesus Christ as the greatest of God's miracles:

---

[2] *SCG*, book IV, chapter 56.

[A] countless crowd of not only simple but also of the wisest men, embraced the Christian faith, which inculcates things surpassing all human understanding, curbs the pleasures of the flesh, and teaches contempt of all worldly things. That the minds of mortal beings should assent to such things, is both the greatest of miracles, and the evident work of divine inspiration, seeing that they despise visible things and desire only those that are invisible.[3]

When a Thomist states that "there is nothing more divine than being made a cooperator with God,"[4] he sees in the Church the incipient realization of what Vatican II presents as the very goal of divine revelation: the communion of men with God,[5] their participation in divine life:[6] "the invisible God, from the fullness of his love, addresses men as his friends, and moves among them, in order to invite and receive them into his own company."[7] The theological tradition associated with St. Thomas Aquinas has merely highlighted the—metaphysical—vision of reality presupposed by the goal and means of divine action, so that the action of grace can be integrated in a unified way into the whole of man's life.

Protestants and Catholics alike desire to proclaim the Glory of God, to sing to the divine majesty, and to give thanks for the salvation offered in Jesus Christ in his

---

[3] *SCG*, book I, chapter 6.

[4] Pseudo-Dionysius, cited by Cajetan (*De fide et operibus adversus Lutheranos,* cap. IX; *In Summ. Theol.,* Ia, q. 44, a. 4, no. IV), which we have already cited above (chapter 7, note 4).

[5] Cf. the quotation of 1 Jn. 1:2–3 at the heart of the prologue at the Constitution *Dei Verbum* (n0. 1).

[6] Cf. *DV* 6: "God wished to manifest and communicate both himself and the eternal decrees of his will concerning the salvation of mankind. He wished, in other words, 'to share with us divine benefits which entirely surpass the power of the human mind to understand.'"

[7] *DV* 2.

Church. All this already constitutes unity, but certain philosophical preconceptions obstruct a common understanding of this shared intention. I would like to suggest, daringly, that not only the cause of unity, but also the very intention of the Reformers, would be better served if it were disengaged from certain philosophical presuppositions which have been partially conditioning it for almost half a millennium, and which limit its fruition. Although this last goal may be difficult to attain, we will at least have contributed to dialogue by furthering an understanding of certain Catholic approaches.

Bibliography

Abbreviations

AAS   *Acta Apostolicae Sedis,* Rome

AS   *Acta Synodalia Sacrosancti Concilii Oecumenici Vaticani II,* Typis Polyglottis Vaticanis, Civitas Vaticana, 1970–

BEM   Faith and Order, *Baptism, Eucharist, Ministry*

CCQLS   Gabriel Biel, *Collectorium circa quattuor libros Sententiarum*

CF   J. Neuner, J. Dupuis, *The Christian Faith*

CIC   *Codex Iuris Canonici,* 1983

CRBEM   Max Thurian, ed., *Churches Respond to BEM*

Denz.   Heinrich Denzinger, *Enchiridion symbolorum definitionum et declarationum de rebus fidei et morum*

DTC   *Dictionnaire de Théologie Catholique,* Paris, 1903–50

DV   Council Vatican II, Constitution on Divine Revelation, *Dei Verbum*

GS   Council Vatican II, Constitution on the Church in the World of the Present Time, *Gaudium et Spes*

Ia   St. Thomas Aquinas, *Summa theologiae,* Prima Pars

Ia IIae   St. Thomas Aquinas, *Summa theologiae,* Prima Secundae

IIa IIae   St. Thomas Aquinas, *Summa theologiae,*
Secunda Secundae

IIIa   St. Thomas Aquinas, *Summa theologiae,* Tertia Pars

In Summ.   Cajetan (Thomas de Vio), *Commentary on St. Thomas
Aquinas' Summa Theologiae*

ICR   John Calvin, *Institutes of the Christian Religion*

JDDJ   Joint Declaration on the Doctrine of Justification

LG   Council Vatican II, Constitution on the Church,
Lumen Gentium

LW   *Luther's Works,* 55 vol.

SCG   St. Thomas Aquinas, *Summa contra Gentiles*

UUS   John Paul II, Encyclical Letter *Ut Unum Sint*

UR   Council Vatican II, Decree on Ecuminism,
Unitatis Redintegratio

WA   Martin Luther, *Kritische Gesamtausgabe*
("Weimarer Ausgabe"), Weimar 1883ss.

Works Cited

Académie Internationale des Sciences Religieuses. *L'éthique: Perspectives proposées par la foi.* Directed by Jean-Louis Leuba. Le point théologique 56. Paris-Louvain-la-Neuve: Beauchesne-Artel, 1993.

Amaldi, Ugo. "Verità dei modelli e delle affermazioni scientifiche." In *La questione della verità: Filosofia, scienze, teologia.* Directed by Vittorio Possenti, 109–24. Rome: Armando Editore, 2003.

Anglican-Reformed International Commission. *God's Reign and Our Unity: The Report of the Anglican-Reformed International Commission 1984.* London: SPCK; Edinburgh: Saint Andrew Press, 1984.

Barr, James. *Biblical Faith and Natural Theology.* New York: Oxford University Press, Clarendon Paperbacks, 1993.

Barth, Karl. Church Dogmatics. Vol. 1, Part 1: *The Doctrine of the Word of God.* Translated by G. T. Thomson. Edinburgh: T&T Clark, 1957.

———. *Church Dogmatics.* Vol. 2, Part 1: The Doctrine of God. Translated by T. H. L. Parker et al. Edited by G. W. Bromiley and T. F. Torrance. Edinburgh: T&T Clark, 1957.

Basset, Jean-Claude. *Le dialogue interreligieux: Histoire et avenir.* Cogitatio Fidei 197. Paris: Cerf, 1996.

Biel, Gabriel. *Collectorium circa quattuor libros sententiarum,* Auspiciis H. Rückert. Edited by W. Werbeck and U. Hofmann. 5 vols. Tübingen: J. C. B. Mohr, 1973–77 (index, 1992).

Birmelé, André "Analyse protestante." In Comité Mixte Catholique-Protestant de France. *Consensus oecuménique et différence fondamentale,* 29–44. Paris: Le Centurion, 1987.

———. *La communion ecclésiale: Progrès oecuméniques et enjeux méthodologiques.* Cogitatio Fidei 218. Paris: Cerf, 2000.

———. *Le Salut en Jésus-Christ dans les dialogues oecuméniques.* Cogitatio Fidei 241. Paris: Cerf; Geneva: Labor et Fides, 1986.

Birmelé, André and Jacques Terme, eds. *Accords et dialogues oecuméniques: Bilatéraux, Multilatéraux, Français, Européens, Internationaux.* Paris: Les Bergers et les Mages, 1995–present (publication updated).

Birmelé, André and Harding Meyer, eds. *Grundkonsens–Grund-differenz: Studie des Straßbuger Institut für oekumenische Forschung.* Frankfurt: Otto Lembeck Verlag; Paderborn: Bonifatius Verlag, 1992.

Blöchle, Herbert. *Luthers Stellung zum Heidentum im Spannungsfeld von Tradition, Humanismus und Reformation.* Frankfurt am Main: Peter Lang, 1995.

Bonansea, Benardino. *L'uomo e Dio nel pensiero di Duns Scoto.* Milan: Jaca Book, 1991.

Bonaventure, Saint. *Breviloquium.* Quaracchi ed., vol. 5.

———. *In Joan.* Quaracchi ed., vol. 6.

Bühler, Pierre. "Origines et développement de l'herméneutique: aperçu sur quelques étapes." *Bulletin de l'Institut de Recherches herméneutiques et systématiques,* Neuchâtel, no. 1 (Sept. 1994): 9–12.

Burkard, Franz-Josef. "Gabriel Biel." In *Lexikon für Theologie und Kirche.* Vol. 2. Freiburg: Herder, 1994.

Cajetan. See Thomas de Vio Cardinalis Caietanus.

Calvin, John, *Institutes of the Christian Religion,* The Library of Christian Classics, vol. XX–XXI, Philadelphia; Westminster Press; London: S.C.M. Press, 1967.

———. *The Geneva Catechism,* http://www.ondoctrine.com/2cal0504.htm.

Capizzi, A. "Anima e corpo nel XIII secolo." *Giornale Critico della Filosofia Italiana* (1951): 24–42, 205–27.

Cassirer, Heinz W. *Grace and Law: St. Paul, Kant and the Hebrew Prophets.* Grand Rapids: Eerdmans, 1988.

Catechism of the Catholic Church. 2nd ed. Vatican City: Libreria Editrice Vaticana for the United States Conference of Catholic Bishops, 1997.

Chantraine, Georges. *Erasme et Luther: Libre et serf arbitre.* Paris: Editions Lethellieux; Namur: Presses Universitaires de Namur, 1981.

Chavannes, Henry. *L'analogie entre Dieu et le monde, selon saint Thomas d'Aquin et selon Karth Barth.* Cogitatio Fidei 42. Paris: Cerf, 1969.

Chevallier, P. *Dionysiaca: Recueil donnant l'ensemble des traductions latines des ouvrages attribués au Denys de l'Aréopage.* Vol. 2. Paris: Desclée de Brouwer, 1950.

Chollet, A. "Cause." In *Dictionnaire de Théologie Catholique.* Paris, vol. II.2, 1910.

Comité Mixte Catholique-Protestant de France. *Consensus oecuménique et différence fondamentale.* Paris: Le Centurion, 1987.

Congar, Yves M.-J. *Martin Luther: Sa foi, sa Réforme.* Cogitatio Fidei 119. Paris: Cerf, 1983.

———. *Tradition and traditions: An Historical and a Theological Essay.* New York, Macmillan, 1966.

———. "Un unique médiateur" (excursus), in Commission Internationale Catholique-Lutherienne, *Face à l'unité,* Tous les textes officiels (1972–85), 271–79. Paris: Cerf, 1986.

Cotta, Gabriella. *La nascita dell'individualismo politico: Lutero e la politica della modernità.* Bologna: Il Mulino, 2002.

Cottier, Georges. *L'athéisme du jeune Marx: Ses origines hégéliennes.* Paris: Vrin, 1959.

Crawford, Patricia A. "Kant and the Refutation of Scepticism." In *Actes du Congrès d'Ottawa sur Kant dans les traditions anglo-américaine et continentale tenu du 10 au 14 octobre 1974,* 344–49. Ottawa: Editions de l'Université d'Ottawa, 1976.

Dettloff, Werner. "Gabriel Biel." In *Theologische Realenzyklopädie.* Vol. 6. Berlin: W. de Gruyter, 1980.

Dieter, Theodor. *Der junge Luther und Aristoteles: Eine historich-systematische Untersuchung zum Verhältnis von Theologie und Philosophie.* Berlin: De Gruyter, 2001.

Dondain, H.-D. "A propos d'Avicenne et de saint Thomas." *Revue Thomiste* 51 (1951): 441–53.

Duns Scotus. See Ioannis Duns Scotus.

Duquoc, Christian. *Des Églises provisoires: Essai d'ecclésiologie oecuménique.* "Théologies." Paris: Cerf, 1985.

———. *Je crois en l'Église: Précarité institutionnelle et Règne de Dieu.* Théologies. Paris: Cerf, 1999.

Ebeling, Gerhard. *Luther: Introduction à une réflexion théologique.* Geneva: Labor et Fides, 1981.

Eiben, Jürgen. *Von Luther zu Kant—Der deutsche Sonderweg in die Moderne: Eine soziologische Betrachtung.* Wiesbaden: Deutscher Universitätsverlag, 1989.

Farthing, John L. "Gabriel Biel." In *Routledge Encyclopedia of Philosophy.* London: Routledge, 1998.

———. *Thomas Aquinas and Gabriel Biel: Interpretation of St. Thomas Aquinas in German Nominalism on the Eve of the Reformation.* Duke Monographs in Medieval and Renaissance Studies 9. London: Duke University Press, 1998.

Fatio, Olivier. "Le Conseil Oecuménique des Eglises doit-il survivre?" In *Pour sortir l'oecuménisme du purgatoire.* Edited by Olivier Fatio and Henry Mottu, 7–18. Publications de la Faculté de Théologie de l'Université de Genève 18. Geneva: Labor et Fides, 1993.

Faith and Order. *Baptism, Eucharist, and Ministry.* Geneva: World Council of Churches, 1982.

Fédération des Églises Protestantes de Suisse. *Lignes directrices de l'action oecuménique,* 1994.

Feyerabend, Paul. *Against Method: Outline of an Anarchistic Theory of Knowledge.* London: Verso, 1988.

———. *Farewell to Reason.* London: Verso, 1987.

———. *Killing Time: The Autobiography of Paul Feyerabend.* Chicago: University of Chicago Press, 1995.

———. *Philosophical Papers.* Cambridge: Cambridge University Press, 1981.

———. *Three Dialogues on Knowledge.* Oxford: Blackwell, 1991.

Flannery, Austin, gen. ed. *Vatican Council II.* Vol. 1: *The Conciliar and Post Conciliar Documents,* new revised ed. Northport, NY: Costello Publishing Company; Dublin: Dominican Publications, 1996.

Fleaux-Mulot, Rachel. "Le croyant et son cerveau: 3 expériences religieuses au microscope." *Sciences et Avenir* (September 2003): 12–13.

Gassman, Günther. "Kirche als Sakrament, Zeichen und Werkzeug. Die Rezeption dieser eccklesiologischen Perspektive in der ökumenischen Diskussion." In *Die Sakramentalität der Kirche in der ökumenischen Diskussion.* Paderborn: éd. Johann Adam, 171–201. Möhler Institut, 1983.

Grane, Leif. *Contra Gabrielem: Luthers Auseinandersetzung mit Gabriel Biel in der Disputatio contra scholasticam theologiam 1517.* Acta theologica danica no. 4. Kopenhagen: Gyldendal, 1962.

Greenberg, Irving, "Seeking the Religious Roots of Pluralism: In the Image of God and Covenant." *Journal of Ecumenical Studies* 34, no. 3 (Summer 1997): 385–94.

Grushow, Gerald. *Science of God.* Virginia Beach: Starway Scientific Press, 2001.

Hennig, Gerhard. *Cajetan und Luthers: Ein historischer Beitrag zur Begegnung von Thomismus und Reformation,* 2nd ed. Vol. 7. Stuttgart: Calwer Verlag, 1966.

Hick, John. *God and the Universe of Faiths: Essays in the Philosophy of Religion.* London: Macmillan, 1973.

Hobbes, Thomas. *De Cive: Philosophicall Rudiments Concerning Government and Society. Or, A Dissertation Concerning Man in his severall habitudes and respects, as the Member of a Society, first Secular, and than Sacred. Containing The Elements of Civill Politie in the Agreement which it hath both with Naturall and Divine Lawes.* Printed by J. C. for R. Royston, at the Angel in Ivie-Lane. London, 1651.

———. *Leviathan,* rev. student ed. Cambridge: Cambridge University Press, 1997.

Institute for Ecumenical Research Strasbourg. *Crisis and Challenge of the Ecumenical Movement: Integrity and Indivisibility, A Statement of the Institute for Ecumenical Research Strasbourg.* Geneva: WCC Publications, 1994.

International Commission for Catholic-Reformed Dialogue. *Towards a Common Understanding of the Church. Information Service,* English ed., 74 (1990): 91–125.

Irenaeus of Lyon, *Against Heresies.* In *The Ante-Nicene Fathers.* Edited by Alexander Roberts and James Donaldson. American reprint of the Edinburgh edition, by A. Cleveland Coxe. Vol. 1. Grand Rapids: Eerdmans, 1985.

Ioannis Duns Scoti. *Opera Omnia*. Vol. 3. Roma: Typis Polyglottis Vaticanis, 1954.

Janz, D. R. "Thomas Aquinas, Martin Luther, and the Origins of the Protestant Reformation." *Medieval Studies* 12 (1991): 71–83.

————. *Luther on Thomas Aquinas: The Angelic Doctor in the Thought of the Reformer.* Frank Steiner Verlag Wiesbaden. Veröffentlichungen des Instituts für europäische Geschichte Mainz. Vol. 140. Stuttgart: Abteilung für abendländliche Religionsgeschichte, 1989.

John Paul II. Encyclical letter *Fides et Ratio*. September 14, 1998.

————. Encyclical letter *Ut Unum Sint*. May 25, 1995.

Joint Declaration on the Doctrine of Justification: The Lutheran World Federation and the Roman Catholic Church. Grand Rapids: Eerdmans, 2000.

Joint Lutheran/Roman Catholic Study Commission. "Church and Justification" (1993), no. 166 in *Information Service* 86, 1994/ii–iii, 159.

————. *Facing Unity: Models, Forms and Phases of Catholic-Lutheran Church Fellowship.* Geneva: Lutheran World Federation, 1985.

————. "The Gospel and the Church" ("Malta Report"), 1972. *Lutheran World* 19, 3 (1972): 259–73.

————. "All Under One Christ" (1980), in *Facing Unity*, no. 14.

Journet, Charles. *Connaissance et inconnaissance de Dieu.* Fribourg: Librarie de l'Université, 1943.

————. *Entretiens sur la grâce.* Saint-Maurice: Éditions S.-Augustin, 1969.

Jüngel, Eberhard. "Um Gottes Willen—Klarheit!" *Zeitschrift für Theologie und Kirche* 94 (1996): 394–406.

————. "Die Kirche als Sakrament?" *Zeitschrift für Theologie und Kirche* 80 (1983): 432–57.

————. *Das Evangelium von der Rechtfertigung des Gottlosen als Zentrum des christlichen Glaubens: Eine theologische Studie in ökumenischer Absicht.* Tübingen: Mohr Siebeck, 1998.

Kant, Immanuel. *The One Possible Basis for a Demonstration of the Existence of God* (1763). Translated by Gordon Treash. Janus Library. New York: Abaris Books, 1979.

———. *Critique of Judgment.* Translated by J. H. Bernard. Hafner Library of Classics 14. New York: Hafner Publishing Co., 1951.

———. *Critique of Practical Reason.* In Great Books of the Western World. Edited by William Benton. Vol. 42. Chicago-London-Toronto: Encyclopaedia Britannica Inc., 1952.

———. *Critique of Pure Reason.* Translated by Norman Kemp Smith. Basingstoke: Palgrave Macmillan, 2003.

———. *On the Failure of All Attempted Philosophical Theodicies* (1791). Translated by Michel Despland. In Michel Despland, *Kant on History and Religion.* Montreal: McGill University Press; London: Queen's University Press, 1973.

———. *Religion within the Limits of Reason Alone.* Translated by Theodore M. Greene and Hoyt H. Hudson. La Salle, IL: Open Court Publishing, 1934; reprint, New York: Harper, Perennial, 1960.

Kasper, Walter. "Le radici teologiche del conflitto tra Mosca e Roma." *La Civiltà Cattolica* 3642 (March 16, 2002): 531–41.

Kinnamon, Michael and Cope, Brian E., eds. *The Ecumenical Movement: An Anthology of Key Texts and Voices.* Geneva: WCC Publications; Grand Rapids: Eerdmans, 1997.

Klein, Laurentius. *Konfessionskundliche und kontroverstheologische Studien.* Vol. 5: *Evangelisch-lutherische Beichte: Lehre und Praxis.* Paderborn: Bonifacius-Druckerei, 1961.

Klinger, Elmar. "Macht und Dialog, Die grundlegende Bedeutung des Pluralismus in der Kirche." In *Dialog als Selbsvollzug der Kirche?* Edited by Gebhard Fürst, 150–65. Freiburg: Herder, 1997.

Kretschmar, Georg. "La foi et l'éthique chez les réformateurs." In Académie Internationale des Sciences Religieuses, *L'éthique: perspectives proposées par la foi.* Directed by Jean Louis Leuba. Le point théologique 56. Paris: Beauchesne; Louvain-la Neuve: Artel, 1993.

Kuhn, Thomas. *The Essential Tension: Studies in Scientific Tradition and Change.* Chicago: University of Chicago Press, 1977.

———. *The Structure of Scientific Revolutions,* 2nd ed. Chicago: University of Chicago Press, 1970.

Lambinet, Ludwig. *Das Wesen des katholisch-protestantischen Gegensatzes: Ein Beitrag zum gegeseitigen Verstehen.* Eisiedeln, Cologne: Benziger, 1946.

Landgraf, A. "Grundlagen für ein Verständnis der Busslehre der Früh- und Hochscholastik." *Zeitschrift für Theologie und Kirche* (1927): 161–94.

Lange, Dietz, and the Göttingen Faculty of Theology. *Ueberholte Verurteilungen? Die Gegensätze in der Lehre von Rechtfertigung, Abendmahl und Amt zwischen dem Konzil von Trient und der Reformation—damals und heute.* Göttingen: Vandenhoeck und Ruprecht, 1991.

Levi, Anthony. *Renaissance and Reformation: The Intellectual Genesis.* London: Yale University Press, 2002.

Lienhard, Marc. Introduction to *Oeuvres,* vol. 1, by Martin Luther. Bibliothèque de la Pléiade. Paris: Gallimard, 1999.

———. *Martin Luther: Un temps, une vie, un message.* 3rd ed. Histoire et Société 21r. Geneva: Labor et Fides, 1991.

Lindbeck, George. "Ecumenical Theology." In *The Modern Theologians: An Introduction to Christian Theology in the Twentieth Century.* Edited by David F. Ford. Vol. 2. Blackwell: Oxford, 1989.

Luther, Martin. *Kritische Gesamtausgabe.* "Weimarer Ausgabe." Weimar 1883ss.

———. *Luther's Works,* 55 vol., St. Louis: Concordia/Philadelphia: Fortress Press, 1957–86.

———. *The Bondage of the Will* (*De servo arbitrio,* 1525), LW 33, 3–295.

———. *Disputation against Scolastic Theology,* LW 31, 3–16.

———. *Heidelberg Disputation* LW 31, 35–42.

———. *Lectures on Romans* LW 25.

———. *Resolutiones disputationum de indulgentiarum virtute,* with their introduction, WA 1, 22–628; English translation:

Explanations of the Disputation Concerning the Value of Indulgences, LW 31, 76–252.

Lutheran-Methodist Joint Commission. *The Church: Community of Grace.* Geneva: Lutheran World Federation; Lake Junaluska, NC: World Methodist Council, 1984.

Montagnes, Bernard. *La doctrine de l'analogie de l'être d'après saint Thomas d'Aquin.* Louvain: Publications universitaires; Paris: Éd. Béatrice-Nauwelaerts, 1963.

Morerod, Charles. *Cajetan et Luther en 1518: Edition, traduction et commentaire des opuscules d'Augsbourg de Cajetan,* 2 vols. Cahiers Oecuméniques 26. Fribourg, Switzerland: Éditions Universitaires, 1994.

———. "La primauté de Pierre." In Boris Bobrinskoy, Patrick Chauvet, et al., *Qu'ils soient un: L'oecuménisme dans le sillage du Père Marie-Joseph Le Guillou.* Paris: Éditions Parole et Silence, 2001.

———. "La relation entre les religions selon John Hick." *Nova et Vetera* 75 (2000): 35–62.

———. "L'infaillibilité du pape selon Jean de Saint-Thomas." *Nova et Vetera* 77, no. 1 (2002): 5–35.

Neuner, J. and J. Dupuis, *The Christian Faith.* 6th rev. and enlarged ed. New York: Alba House, 1996

Newberg, Andrew, Eugene d'Aquili, and Vincent Rause. *Why God Won't Go Away: Brain Science and the Biology of Belief.* New York: Ballantine Books, 2001.

Nicolas, Jean-Hervé. "L'origine première des choses." *Revue Thomiste* 91 (1991): 181–218.

———. *Dieu connu comme inconnu.* Paris: Desclée de Bouwer, 1966.

Nietzsche, Friedrich. *Thus Spake Zarathustra.* Translated by Thomas Common. eBooks@Adelaide, 2004.

O'Callaghan, Paul. *Fides Christi: The Justification Debate.* Dublin: Four Court Press, 1997.

O'Donnell, Christopher. *Ecclesia: A Theological Encyclopedia of the Church.* Collegeville: Michael Glazier, Liturgical Press, 1996.

Oberman, Heiko Augustinus. *The Harvest of Medieval Theology: Gabriel Biel and Late Medieval Nominalism,* rev. ed. Grand Rapids: Eerdmans, 1967.

Outler, A. C. "Protestant Observer at Vatican II Surveys Ecumenism." *Origins* 16, no. 14 (1986): 253–57.

Paul VI. Encyclical letter *Ecclesiam Suam.* August 6, 1964.

Pelikan, Jaroslav. *La Tradition chrétienne: Histoire du développement de la doctrine.* Vol. 4: *La réforme de l'Église et du dogme.* Théologiques. Paris: PUF, 1984.

Pesch, Otto Hermann. *Hinführung zu Luther.* Mainz: Matthias-Grünewald-Verlag, 1982.

————. *Die Theologie der Rechtfertigung bei Martin Luther und Thomas von Aquin: Versuch eines systematisch-theologischen Dialogs.* Walberberger Studien 4. Mainz: Matthias-Grünewald-Verlag, 1967.

————. *Thomas d'Aquin: Grandeur et limites de la théologie médiévale.* Cogitatio Fidei 177. Paris: Cerf, 1994.

Peter, Carl J. "A Moment of Truth for Lutheran-Catholic Dialogue." *Origins* 17, no. 31 (1988): 537–41.

Popper, Karl. *All Life Is Problem Solving: Questions about the Knowledge of Nature.* London: Routledge, 1999.

————. *The Lesson of This Century.* London: Routledge, 1996.

————. *The Logic of Scientific Discovery.* London: Hutchinson, 1959.

————. *Objective Knowledge: An Evolutionary Approach.* Oxford: Clarendon Press, 1972.

————. *The Open Society and Its Enemies.* 2 vols. London: Routledge, 1945.

————. *Unended Quest: An Intellectual Autobiography,* rev. ed. Glasgow: Fontana, 1976.

Radner, Ephraim, and Russell R. Reno. *Inhabiting Unity: Theological Perspectives on the Proposed Lutheran-Episcopal Concordat.* Grand Rapids: Eerdmans, 1995.

Sertillanges, A. D. Appendix "Prédestination." In St. Thomas Aquinas, *Somme théologique.* La Revue des Jeunes ed., Vol. 3. Paris: Desclée; Rome: Tournai, 1926, 321–26.

Sesboüé, Bernard. *Pour une théologie oecuménique.* Paris: Cerf, 1990.

———. "Analyse catholique." In Comité Mixte Catholique-Protestant de France. *Consensus oecuménique et différence fondamentale.* Paris: Le Centurion, 1987.

"Stellungnahme theologischer Hochschullehrer zur geplanten Unterzeichnung der Gemeinsamen Offiziellen Feststellung zur Rechtfertigungslehre." In *Materialdienst des Konfessionskundlichen Instituts Bensheim,* no. 6 (1999): 114–15.

Süss, Théobald. *Luther.* Philosophes. Paris: Presses Universitaires de France, 1969.

Theological Faculty, Georgia Augusta University, Göttingen. "An Opinion on the Condemnations of the Reformation Era." *Lutheran Quarterly* 5, no. 1 (1991): 1–62; 5, no. 3 (1991): 337–71; 5, no. 4 (1991): 493–512.

Thomas Aquinas, *The Summa Theologica of St. Thomas Aquinas.* Translated by Fathers of the English Dominican Province, Great Books of the Western World, Chicago-London-Toronto: Encyclopedia Britannica, 1952.

———. *The Summa contra Gentiles.* Translated by the English Dominican Fathers from the Latest Leonine Edition. 2 vols. London: Burns Oates and Washbourne, 1923–24.

Thomas de Vio Cardinalis Caietanus. *Instructio nuntii circa errores libelli de Cena Domini sive De erroribus contingentibus in Eucharistiae sacramento,* no. 42. Franciscus A. von Gunten OP editionem curavit. Rome: Apud Pontificium Athenaeum "Angelicum," 1962.

———. *Commentary on St. Thomas Aquinas' Summa Theologiae.* In *Sancti Thomae Aquinatis Doctoris Angelici Opera Omnia iussu impensaque Leonis XIII P.M. edita.* Typographia polyglotta, tt.IV–XII. Rome, 1898–06.

Thurian, Max, ed. *Churches Respond to BEM.* 6 vols. Geneva: World Council of Churches, 1986–88.

Tillich, Paul, *The Protestant Era* (Abridged). Translated by James Luther Adams. Chicago: University of Chicago Press, 1957.

————. "The Permanent Significance of the Catholic Church for Protestantism." *Protestant Digest* 3, no. 10 (1941): 23–31.

————. *Systematic Theology.* Vol.3: *Life and the Spirit, History and the Kingdom of God.* Chicago: University of Chicago Press, 1963.

Tillard, Jean-Marie R. "Vers une nouvelle problématique de la 'justification.'" *Irénikon* 55 (1982): 185–98.

Tracy, David. *The Analogical Imagination: Christian Theology and the Culture of Pluralism.* New York: Crossroad, 1987.

United States Joint Group for Lutheran-Catholic Dialogue. *Justification by Faith.* Edited by T. George Anderson, T. Austin Murphy, and Joseph A. Burgess. Lutherans and Catholics in Dialogue 7. Minneapolis: Augsburg Publishing House, 1985.

Vischer, Lukas, ed. *A Documentary History of the Faith and Order Movement, 1927–1963.* St. Louis: Bethany Press, 1963.

"Votum der Hochschullehrer zur 'Gemeinsamen Erklärung zur Rechtfertigungslehre' vom Januar 1998." *Materialdienst des Konfessionskundlichen Instituts Bensheim,* no. 2 (1998): 33–35.

Wicks, Jared. *Cajetan Responds: A Reader in Reformation Controversy* (Washington, DC: Catholic University of America Press, 1978).

————. *Cajetan und die Anfänge der Reformation.* Katholisches Leben und Kämpfen im Zeitalter der Glaubensspaltung. Vereinsschriften der Gesselschaft zur Herausgabe des Corpus Catholicorum 43 (aus dem englischen Manuskript übersetzt von Barbara Hallensleben).

Williams, Rowan. "Eastern Orthodox Theology." In *The Modern Theologians: An Introduction to Christian Theology in the Twentieth Cenetury.* Edited by David F. Ford. Vol. 2. Blackwell: Oxford, 1989.

Index

Catholic-Reformed Dialogue,
    133–35
Tracy, David, 35
transcendence. *See* divine
    majesty and transcendence
Trent, Council of (1547), 59,
    137–38, 146